The **AA POCKET**Guide
CORFU

Corfu: Regions and Best places to see

Original text by Des Hannigan
Updated by Des Hannigan

© Automobile Association Developments Limited 2008
First published 2008
Reprinted July 2008

ISBN: 978-0-7495-5504-7

Published by AA Publishing, a trading name of Automobile Association Developments
Limited, whose registered office is Fanum House, Basing View, Basingstoke, Hampshire
RG21 4EA. Registered number 1878835.

Colour separation: Keenes, Andover
Printed and bound in Italy by Printer Trento S.r.l.

Front cover image (t) AA/J A Tims; (b) AA/C Sawyer
Back cover image: AA/C Sawyer

A03876
Maps in this title produced from mapping © Freytag-Berndt u. Artaria KG,
1231 Vienna-Austria

About this book

Symbols are used to denote the following categories:

➕ map reference

✉ address or location

☎ telephone number

🕐 opening times

💷 admission charge

🍴 restaurant or café on premises or nearby

Ⓜ nearest underground train station

🚌 nearest bus/tram route

🚉 nearest overground train station

⛴ nearest ferry stop

✈ nearest airport

↔ other places of interest nearby

❓ other practical information

➤ indicates the page where you will find a fuller description

This book is divided into four sections.

Planning pages 6–19
Before You Go; Getting There; Getting Around; Being There

Best places to see pages 20–41
The unmissable highlights of any visit to Corfu

Exploring pages 42–123
The best places to visit in Corfu, organized by area

Maps pages 127–144
All map references are to the atlas section. For example, Kérkyra has the reference ➕ 133 B7 – indicating the page number and grid square in which it is to be found

Contents

Planning

Before You Go

WHEN TO GO

JAN	FEB	MAR	APR	MAY	JUN	JUL	AUG	SEP	OCT	NOV	DEC
14°C	15°C	16°C	19°C	23°C	28°C	31°C	32°C	28°C	23°C	19°C	16°C
57°F	59°F	61°F	66°F	73°F	82°F	88°F	90°F	82°F	73°F	66°F	61°F

🔵 High season ⚪ Low season

May and June are good times to visit, when the temperature starts to climb but it isn't too hot and the island is not yet too busy with visitors. Those interested in wild flowers, and who don't mind the risk of occasional showers, should consider April. In July and August it is hot and there is very little rain, although even then you may get some showers. Corfu is one of the greenest of the Greek islands, and it can rain at any time. The holiday season runs from Easter until October, and outside this period many hotels and restaurants will be closed. There are still many open all year round, but your choices will be more limited. Corfu does not make for a good winter holiday, although Corfu Town provides an under-rated city break destination.

WHAT YOU NEED

●	Required	Some countries require a passport to remain valid for a minimum period (usually at least six months) beyond the date of entry – contact their consulate or embassy or your travel agent for details.
○	Suggested	
▲	Not required	

	UK	Germany	USA	Netherlands	Spain
Passport (or National Identity Card where applicable)	●	●	●	●	▲
Visa (regulations can change – check before you travel)	▲	▲	▲	▲	▲
Onward or Return Ticket	▲	▲	▲	▲	▲
Health Inoculations (tetanus and polio)	○	○	○	○	○
Health Documentation (▶ 9, Health Advice)	●	●	▲	●	▲
Travel Insurance	●	●	●	●	●
Driving Licence (national)	●	●	●	●	●
Car Insurance Certificate	●	●	●	●	●
Car Registration Document	●	●	▲	●	●

ADVANCE PLANNING
WEBSITES
- www.culture.gr
- www.gnto.gr
- www.ktel.org
- www.corfuonline.gr
- www.greeka.com/ionian/corfu/island/travel-corfu.htm
- www.agni.gr
- www.corfunews.net
- www.pelekas.com

TOURIST OFFICES AT HOME
In the UK Greek National Tourist Organisation (GNTO) ✉ 4 Conduit Street, London, W1R 0DJ ☎ 020 7734 5997

In the USA Greek National Tourist Organisation (GNTO) ✉ Olympic Tower, 645 5th Avenue, New York, NY 10022 ☎ 212/421-5777

In Canada Greek National Tourism Organisation (GNTO) ✉ 91 Scollard Street, Toronto, Ontario, M5R 1GR ☎ 416/968-2220

In Australia Greek National Tourism Organisation (GNTO) ✉ 51–57 Pitt Street, Sydney, NSW 2000 ☎ (02) 9241 1663

HEALTH ADVICE
Insurance Visitors from EU countries are entitled to reciprocal state medical care in Greece and should take an EHIC – European Health Insurance Card. However, this covers treatment in only the most basic of hospitals and private medical insurance is advisable.

Dental services Dental treatment must be paid for by all visitors. Hotels can normally provide you with the name of a local English-speaking dentist; alternatively you could ask the Tourist Police or a tourist office. Private medical insurance is strongly advisable to cover dental treatment.

TIME DIFFERENCES

| GMT 12 noon | Corfu 2PM | Germany 1PM | USA (NY) 7AM | Netherlands 1PM | Spain 1PM |

Corfu, like the whole of Greece, is two hours ahead of Greenwich Mean Time (GMT+2) and adjusts to summertime at 4am on the last Sunday in March until 4am on the last Sunday in October.

WHAT'S ON WHEN

January 1 January – *New Year's Day*.
6 January – *Epiphany*. Religious ceremonies held.

February–March *Pre-Lenten Carnival*. During the three weeks before the start of Lent, carnivals take place at various villages on Corfu. On the Sunday before Lent (seven Sundays before Easter) there is a big carnival procession in Corfu Town.
Kathari Deftera (Clean Monday) – the Monday after Carnival Sunday and before Ash Wednesday. Public holiday in Greece. On Corfu it is celebrated by families and friends with huge picnics. Kite flying.
8 March – *St Theodora's Day*. The saint's remains are carried around Corfu Town.
25 March – *Independence Day* and *Feast of the Annunciation*.

April *Easter* (movable). The most important celebration of the Greek year. A genuine rebirth. On Corfu, numerous religious services are held during the preceding Holy Week.
Palm Sunday – the remains of St Spyrídon are carried in procession through Corfu Town.
Good Friday – numerous church processions through Corfu Town and at villages.
Easter Saturday – procession from Church of St Spyrídon. Pot throwing custom (➤ opposite). Atmospheric late evening candle-lit ceremony of the Resurrection on the Esplanade. Fireworks display.
Easter Sunday – Resurrection parades from churches in Corfu Town and villages. Countless fairs. throughout the island.

May 1 May – *Labour day*.
Festival at Róda and on Mount Ágios Déka, and family picnics throughout the island.
4 May – *Feast of St Thomas*. festivals at Sidári, Gastoúri and Benítses, among others.
8 May – festival at Kassiópi.
21 May – *Ionian Day*. Annual celebration of the Ionian Islands union with Greece in 1864. Local holiday. Procession in Corfu Town. Brass band display on the Esplanade.

NATIONAL HOLIDAYS

JAN	FEB	MAR	APR	MAY	JUN	JUL	AUG	SEP	OCT	NOV	DEC
2	(1)	1(2)	(1)	1	1		1		1		2

1 Jan	New Year's Day
6 Jan	Epiphany
End Feb/early Mar	*Kathari Deftera* (Clean Monday)
25 Mar	Independence Day
Mar/Apr	Holy Week Celebrations
1 May	Labour Day
3 Jun	Holy Spirit Day
15 Aug	Feast of the Assumption
28 Oct	Óchi Day
25 Dec, 26 Dec	Christmas Day, St Stephen's Day

The Feast of St Spyridon (11 Aug) is an unofficial public holiday. Shops and some restaurants close on public holidays. In Corfu Town and in main resorts, tavernas and most shops stay open.

June *Pentecost Sunday* – festival at Lákones.
Whit Monday – festivals at Kondókali, Stavros and Argirádes, among others.

July 8 July – *St Prokopios's Day*. Festival at Lefkímmi.
26 July – *St Paraskevi's Day*. Festivals at Ágios Matthéos, Ipsos, Avliótes, Benítses, Kinopiastes.

August 6 August – *Saviour's Day*. During the preceding week there are pilgrimages to the top of Mount Pandokrator (➤ 40–41). Festivals in Campiello district of Corfu Town, Ágios Matthéos and Strinýlas.
11 August – *St Spyrídon's Day*. Big procession of casket holding saint's remains through Corfu Town.

15 August – *Assumption of the Virgin*. National holiday. Corfiots traditionally return to home villages. Festivals at Platitéra Monastery (➤ 69) and at numerous villages.

Pot throwing
At 11am on Holy Saturday morning the custom of pot throwing takes place, involving large earthenware pots, sometimes filled with water, being dropped from windows and high balconies in Corfu Town. Pots are also smashed in villages. There are numerous explanations, ranging from it being a reference to Judas's betrayal of Christ for a pot of gold, to the joy of the Virgin Mary at discovering Christ's tomb to be empty, to prehistoric rituals of pottery breaking at burials.

Getting There

BY AIR

There are no direct scheduled flights to Corfu from airports outside Greece although rumours are always rife about various carriers being 'in discussion' about establishing a direct service from one or other Northern European airport, including British ones. It is worth checking general flight websites to see whether or not this much rumoured service has become a reality.

Scheduled services Current scheduled services operate via Athens where they connect with the regular daily internal flights to the island. These take about 1 hour and are operated by the Greek national carrier, Olympic Airways (☎ 26610-38694; **www.**olympic-airways.gr) or the privately operated Aegean Airlines (☎ 26610-27100; **www.**aegeanair.com). Olympic also operates three flights per week between Corfu and Greece's second city, Thessaloníki.

Seaplanes A seaplane service, run by AirSea Lines (☎ 26610-49800 Corfu Town; 26610-99316 Gouviá Marina; **www.**airsealines.com) using 19-seater De Havilland Twin

Otters, operates daily flights between Igoumenítsa on the Greek mainland and Gouviá in Corfu. The company also operates daily flights between Gouviá and Paxos. At the time of writing, future developments included the possibility of flights between Corfu and Brindisi in Italy.

Charter flights In the summer holiday season there are numerous direct charter flights from many European countries to Corfu, the season usually running from Easter until October.

Holiday companies will offload unsold charter flights via the internet or high-street travel agents,

Pátras on the Greek mainland, which is a useful connection if combining a visit to Corfu with other parts of Greece.

The most regular services from the Greek mainland are from Igoumenítsa to Corfu Town, with at least one car ferry per hour during the day, all year round, and even more frequently in summer. The journey takes under 2 hours on the larger ferries and just over an hour on the smaller ones.

There are also the more expensive passenger-only Flying Dolphin hydrofoils which make the trip in 40 minutes. There are less frequent ferries from Igoumenítsa to Lefkímmi in southern Corfu with a journey-time of one hour.

For general ferry schedules, **www.**gtp.gr is a good website.

It's 1.5km (1 mile) from New Port Ferry Terminal to Corfu Town.

and it is fairly easy to pick up cheap flights to Corfu outside the peak summer months. In July and August flight availability will depend on how well holiday bookings are going that year.

Corfu Airport (☎ 26610-30180) is about 3km (2 miles) to the south of Corfu Town (Kérkyra).

BY SEA
There are ferry connections to Corfu from five ports in Italy, including Venice, but the closest and most frequent services are from Brindisi.

Some of these Italian ferries stop at Corfu on their journey to and from

BY BUS
Getting to an island by bus might not seem the obvious option, but there are daily bus services from Athens to Corfu, which take about 10–11 hours and reach the island on the ferry service from the mainland port at Igoumenítsa.

Getting Around

DRIVING

Driving is on the right. Speed limit on national highways: **100kph (62mph)**. Outside built-up areas: **90kph (56mph)**. Built-up areas: **50kph (31mph)**. Seatbelts must be worn in front seats and in the rear where fitted. Children under 10 years are not allowed in the front seat. Random breath testing takes place. Never drive under the influence of alcohol.

Super and unleaded petrol and diesel are all available. There are few petrol stations in rural areas and they tend to be the most expensive. They open daily (morning only) but may close on Sunday. Cash payment is preferred in rural stations. A useful word is *yemitse* (fill).

It is compulsory to carry a first-aid kit, a fire extinguisher and a warning triangle. Tourists with proof of AA/RAC or similar membership are given free roadside assistance from ELPA, the Greek motoring club. If your vehicle breaks down, dial 104. There are good repair shops in big towns but in rural areas petrol stations can usually find a local mechanic.

INTERNAL FLIGHTS

Domestic flights are operated by Olympic Airways (☎ 26610-38694; **www**.olympic-airlines.com) and Aegean Airlines (☎ 26610-27100; **www**.aegeanair.com), and it is possible to make connections at Athens to Corfu. A seaplane service, run by AirSea Lines operates from Gouviá Marina to Igoumenítsa on the mainland and from Gouviá to Paxos (➤ 12).

ISLAND BUSES

Corfu's rural bus service is run by the national bus company, KTEL (Kratiko Tamio Ellinikon Leoforion). All services start from and return to

Corfu Town. Timetables may be subject to change. Buses can be boarded anywhere along country roads, and tickets are purchased on board. KTEL buses also run between Corfu and Athens. The KTEL terminus in Corfu Town is at the northwest end of Avramiou. For more information ☎ 26610-30627/39985.

FERRIES

Ferries run between Corfu Town and Igoumenítsa on the mainland at half-hourly intervals in winter, and as frequently as 15-minute intervals in summer. Ferries also run at hourly intervals between Lefkímmi and Igoumenítsa. International ferries run between Bari and Brindisi in Italy and Patras on the Greek mainland, calling at Corfu Town. Ferry connections between Corfu and Paxos are uncertain and should be checked.

URBAN TRANSPORT

Blue buses (☎ 26610-39859) operate from San Rocco Square to the suburbs and Gastoúri (Achílleion), Kondókali, Gouviá, Dassiá, Pérama, Benítses, Pélekas, Kanóni, and central Corfu. Pay on board or, for buses marked *horis eispraktor* (without conductor) buy tickets at the kiosk by the San Rocco bus rank.

TAXIS

Call radio cabs (☎ 26610-33811/2). Taxi ranks in Corfu Town are at San Rocco Square, the Esplanade and New Port. Meters should display the fare; if not make sure you determine the cost beforehand. Double rates apply outside Corfu Town.

CAR AND MOTORCYCLE RENTAL

Make sure you have Collision Damage Waiver. However, even

with CDW you are liable for damage to tyres and undercarriage, so do not drive conventional vehicles off-road. Always check the wheels, bodywork and interior of the vehicle in the presence of the hirer before accepting the vehicle. If there is existing damage, make sure that the hirer acknowledges this. Visitors are strongly advised not to consume any alcohol if intending to drive. The minimum rental age is from 21 to 25.

Being There

TOURIST OFFICES

Visitors should note that Greek National Tourism Organization (GNTO) is the title used outside Greece. In Greece it is known as Ellinikos Organismos Tourismou (EOT).

ATHENS

● Greek National Tourism Organization (GNTO), Head Office Tsoha 7, Ambelokipi, Athens 11521 ☎ (210) 870 7000

● GNTO Central Information Office, Amalias 26a, Syntagma, Athens ☎ (210) 331 0392

CORFU TOURIST INFORMATION

● The EOT has closed its Corfu Town office and currently has an office outside town on Eth Antistasseos, which has little information. Tourist information kisoks may be opened in Corfu Town but details are not confirmed at time of writing. Website: **www.**gnto.gr

The Tourist Police (☎ 26610-30265) should be contacted if visitors have difficulties with accommodation or with service.

A friendly reliable agency in Corfu Town that will give some information and arrange accommodation, tours and more for a fee is: **All Ways Travel,** 35 G Theotoki Square ☎ 26610-33955

EMBASSIES AND CONSULATES

UK ☎ 26610-30055/23457
USA/Canada ☎ (210) 721 2951 (Athens)
Germany ☎ 26610-31453
Australia ☎ (210) 645 0404 (Athens)
Netherlands ☎ 26610-39900
Italy ☎ 26610-37351

EMAIL AND INTERNET

Corfu Town has several internet cafés including Netoikos, 14 Kaloxairetou (behind The Liston) ☎ 26610-28637 and Café Online, 28 Kapodistriou (just up from Arcadion Hotel) ☎ 26610-46226. A few of the larger resorts also have internet cafés, usually open until midnight or 1am.

TELEPHONES

To make a call from a street phone you must have an OTE (the national phone company) phone card *(telekarte).* These can be bought for

OPENING HOURS

- Shops
- Offices
- Banks
- Post Offices
- Museums/Monuments
- Pharmacies

| 9 AM | 10 AM | 11 AM | 12 PM | 1 PM | 2 PM | 3 PM | 4 PM | 5 PM | 6 PM |

In addition to the above times (a guide only), supermarkets and gift shops, particularly in resorts, often stay open until 9 or 10pm.

Pharmacies are closed on Saturday and Sunday. Check opening times of museums and sites locally as they vary from summer to winter.

a few euros at small local shops, souvenir shops and, chiefly, at *periptera*, the street kiosks that sell everything from cigarettes to magazines. You can also use the OTE office in Corfu Town (Mantzarou 3), which is better value for international calls. Travel agencies in smaller towns often offer direct dialing facilities. For the domestic operator dial 151, and for the international operator dial 161.

EMERGENCY TELEPHONE NUMBERS

Police 100
Fire 199
Forest fire 191
Ambulance 166
Tourist police 26610-30265

INTERNATIONAL DIALLING CODES

Dial 00 followed by:
UK: 44
USA/Canada: 1
Ireland: 353
Australia: 61
Germany: 49

POSTAL SERVICES

The main post office in Corfu Town is at the junction of Alexandras and Zafiropoulou streets; it's open Mon–Fri 7.30am–8pm.

TOILETS

There are very few public toilets in Corfu. Tavernas and restaurants must have them by law.

ELECTRICITY

The power supply throughout Greece is 220 volts AC, 50 Hz. Sockets accept two-round-pin Continental-style plugs. Visitors from the UK will need a plug adaptor and US visitors will need a voltage transformer.

CURRENCY AND FOREIGN EXCHANGE

Currency The monetary unit in Corfu and throughout Greece is the euro (€). Notes are in denominations of €5, 10, 20, 50, 100, 200 and 500, with coins for 1 and 2 euros, and 1, 2, 5, 10, 20 and 50 cents.

Exchange Cash and travellers' cheques can be exchanged in banks, at exchange bureaux and often in travel agencies and tourist information centres. In small resorts the travel agencies may be your only option as there are only banks in Corfu Town and some of the larger resorts. Banks generally give better exchange rates although commission charges are not standardized so shop around for the best deal. Post offices in Greece no longer offer currency exchange facilities.

Credit cards These are widely accepted in hotels, shops and many restaurants, but a few of the eating places recommended in this guide will only take cash so don't rely totally on plastic. You will need a credit card if you wish to rent a car. There are ATMs in all major resorts, but if staying in a smaller place it is wise to check first.

HEALTH AND SAFETY

Sun advice During the months of May to September, when the sun is

TIPS/GRATUITIES

Yes ✓ No ✗		
Restaurants (service included)	✓	10% or change
Cafés/bars (if service not included)	✓	10%
Taxis	✓	change
Tour guides	✓	€4
Porters	✓	€2 per bag
Chambermaids	✓	discretionary
Restroom attendants	✓	50 cents
Hairdressers	✓	10%

at its hottest, a hat, strong-protection suncream and plenty of water are recommended. Try to keep out of the midday sun.

Drugs Prescription and non-prescription drugs are widely available at pharmacies, indicated by a Green Cross, and they usually have someone who can speak English. When closed each should carry a notice of the nearest open pharmacy, or ring 107 to find out. Bring sufficient supplies of any medication with you, especially if staying in smaller resorts. Also bring prescriptions, indicating generic and not brand names, in case you need more. Codeine is banned in Greece, so check your medical supplies to avoid falling foul of the law.

Safe water Tap water is chlorinated and is regarded as safe.

PHOTOGRAPHY

What to photograph: ancient sites (photography is free for hand held cameras on most sites), villages, parades, harbours. The Greek people like being photographed, but it is polite to ask permission. Where you need permission: in some museums and always if using a tripod. Never photograph near military installations.

CLOTHING SIZES

France	UK	Rest of Europe	USA	
46	36	46	36	
48	38	48	38	
50	40	50	40	
52	42	52	42	
54	44	54	44	**Suits**
56	46	56	46	
41	7	41	8	
42	7.5	42	8.5	
43	8.5	43	9.5	
44	9.5	44	10.5	
45	10.5	45	11.5	**Shoes**
46	11	46	12	
37	14.5	37	14.5	
38	15	38	15	
39/40	15.5	39/40	15.5	
41	16	41	16	
42	16.5	42	16.5	**Shirts**
43	17	43	17	
36	8	34	6	
38	10	36	8	
40	12	38	10	
42	14	40	12	
44	16	42	14	**Dresses**
46	18	44	16	
38	4.5	38	6	
38	5	38	6.5	
39	5.5	39	7	
39	6	39	7.5	
40	6.5	40	8	**Shoes**
41	7	41	8.5	

Best places to see

1

Achilleío
(Achilleion Palace)

Corfu's famous Achilleion Palace is an entertaining example of rather florid neoclassicism and self-indulgence, but all of it set within beautiful surroundings.

The Achilleion, a fascinating relic of 19th-century grand design and occasional kitsch, stands on tree-clad heights above the east coast resort of

Benítses, adjacent to the village of Gastoúri. It was conceived by the Empress Elizabeth of Austria as a tribute to her spiritual hero Achilles, and the result is a confection of colonnades and stucco work based on the classical elegance of Pompeii, the whole crowded with statues, paintings and 19th-century furnishings. Six years after the palace was completed in 1892, the Empress was killed by an assassin on the quayside of Lake Geneva. In 1908 the palace was bought by Kaiser Wilhelm II, who added his own grandiose touches before leaving Corfu in 1914 for more pressing engagements. Eventually taken over by the Greek state, the Achilleion lay unused until it was converted into a casino in 1963.

On view is the ornately decorated entrance hall, the Empress's chapel, and ground-floor reception rooms containing furnishings and memorabilia of the Empress and the Kaiser. In the terraced gardens are numerous statues including the Empress's favourite, the sentimental 'Dying Achilles', and the Kaiser's contribution, an outrageously monumental 'Achilles Triumphant'.

➕ 133 D6 ✉ Gastoúri village. Signposted from Corfu Town and from the coast road north of Benítses ☎ 26610-56245 🕐 Jun–Aug daily 9–7; Sep–May daily 9–3.30 ✋ Expensive 🍴 Cafés (€€) near entrance 🚌 Blue bus 10 from San Rocco Square, Corfu Town ❓ Limited roadside parking only. Very crowded during Jul and Aug

2 Ágios Spyrídonas (Church of St Spyrídon)

Ágios Spyrídonas is the most famous church in Corfu. Built in 1590 to house the sacred relics of St Spyrídon, the patron saint of Corfu and a focus of devotion on the island, where he is known simply as 'The Saint', it is a place of pilgrimage to this day.

Spyrídon (AD270–c348) was a Cypriot bishop, said to have performed numerous miracles. During the 7th century, the saint's revered remains were transferred from Cyprus to Constantinople, but, on the fall of the city in 1453, his body was brought, eventually, to Corfu by an itinerant priest. St Spyrídon is associated with several events which are said to have saved the island from plague, famine and Turkish siege and these are celebrated with solemn, but colourful, processions in which his remains are carried through Corfu Town.

The tall, red-domed bell-tower of the Church of St Spyrídon, reminiscent of the tower of San Giorgio dei Greci in Venice, is a landmark of central Corfu Town. Plain exterior walls hide a lavish interior: there is a superb iconostasis (a screen of white Cycladian marble); silver thuribles (censers) and candelabra crowd the basilica; and a wealth of paintings and icons decorate the walls.

In spite of the steady procession of the faithful – and the merely curious – which passes across the pink-and-white flagstones and through the doors to either side, there is a subdued atmosphere inside the church. Candles still flicker in the gloom 'like yellow crocuses', as described by Gerald Durrell in his reminiscences of a Corfu childhood. Young and old, the plain and the fashionable pay homage to the saint.

The real focus of the church, however, is the ornate casket containing the mummified remains of the saint. These are exposed annually on 12 December (St Spyrídon's Day), at Easter, and on 11 August. The saint's feet are clad in embroidered slippers, which devotees claim become worn because of Spyrídon's frequent night-time wanderings round the Old Town. The casket, silver-coated and bearing 12 enamel medallions, is situated to the right of the altar, within a separate chapel, beneath lamps and votive offerings from which dangle tiny silver ships and other motifs. Only a few steps take you from the dazzling sunshine of the outside world into this intense focus of Greek Orthodoxy.

✚ 136 B3 ✉ Ayiou Spiridonas Street, Corfu Town. Also reached from Plateía Iroon Kypriakou Agonos (St Spyrídon's Square) 🕐 Daily 9–2. Casual visits during services are best avoided 🎟 Free, donations welcome 🍴 Café Plakada (€€) in St Spyrídon's Square ❓ Sober clothing should be worn

3 Angelókastro

The 12th-century ruin of the Byzantine fortress of Angelókastro occupies a spectacular hilltop on the west coast.

Angelókastro is one of the finest historic sites on Corfu. Fortified in the 12th century, it may later have been named after the Byzantine family of Angeloi Komneni, which ruled Corfu during the 11th and 12th centuries. The fortress played a key role in the successful defence of the island for hundreds of years, as from it, a watch could be kept on the vulnerable west coast and signals exchanged with Corfu Town. Angelókastro's greatest test came when several thousand islanders withstood sieges by Turkish invaders in 1537, 1571 and 1716. Its military use ended in the 19th century during the British Protectorate.

The ruins of the fortress stand on top of a rocky pinnacle whose cliffs drop 300m (985ft) into the sea. Cobbled steps wind steeply from a car park to a narrow entrance into the inner keep, above which is the upper keep, crowned by the tiny Church of the Archangels Michael and Gabriel.

Just east of the summit, and at a lower level, are the remains of underground water cisterns. In the lower keep, on the far left of the entrance, is a remarkable hermitage – a cave that was converted into a chapel to St Kyriaki in the late 18th century. Wall-paintings of the Virgin and Christ survive.

✚ 128 F3 ✉ Kríni, just west of Makrádes (follow signs)
and 28km (17 miles) from Corfu Town ◷ May–Sep daily
8.30–3 🍴 Castelo St Angelo Taverna (€€) beside car park
🚌 Green bus from Avramiou Street, Corfu Town–Makrádes,
then 2.5km (1.5-mile) walk ✋ Inexpensive ❓ Take care
near the unprotected cliff edges. The entrance gate is
halfway up the approach steps and is usually locked in
winter and sometimes early and late in the season, if the
ticket kiosk is unattended. Access is not feasible for those
with limited mobility

4 Campiello: Old Corfu Town

The old part of Corfu Town is known as Campiello. It lies behind the seafront between the Old and New fortresses.

Venetian is the emphatic style of Campiello's buildings and its fascinating maze of narrow streets, the *kandounia*, which spreads between the main thoroughfares; lanes are often linked by stone stairways *(skalinades)*, and by vaulted passageways. The original buildings of the medieval town, which developed on the cramped peninsula as a domestic adjunct to the Old Fortress, eventually replacing it as the administrative centre of the island, are long gone. Here, the Venetians built grand Renaissance houses three or four storeys high, which were added to in later centuries to accommodate a growing population within the town walls.

Venetian motifs survive on the sometimes crumbling façades of these wonderful old buildings and on the doorcases, or *portonia*, with their distinctive mouldings. Throughout the day the sun weaves an intricate pattern of shifting light on the walls and turns them to burnished gold in the evening. In the narrow, sun-dappled canyons of Campiello, lines of washing hang like banners between the upper windows, and the mottled walls rise cliff-like past railed balconies and stone pediments to a final blue ribbon of sky. Underfoot, the ground is smoothly paved, and intriguing courtyards, terraced gardens, ancient churches and shrines appear round every other corner. There are neighbourhood shops, cafés, tavernas, bars and workplaces where Corfiots busy themselves with trade and craft. In the mellow evenings, you may catch the sound of musicians practising in the club rooms of the town's four brass bands.

➕ 136 A3 🍴 Numerous cafés, tavernas and restaurants throughout the Old Town

5 Kalámi

Kalámi lies on Corfu's northeast coast, amid a landscape of quiet bays backed by the tree-clad slopes of Mount Pandokrator.

In the famous White House at Kalámi, the writer Lawrence Durrell lived for a time and drew on his impressions for his lyrical book *Prospero's Cell*. Today, Kalámi's idyllic peace and quiet, the 'charms

LAWRENCE DURRELL
(1912 – 1990)

of seclusion' described so vividly by Durrell, are no more. Seen from the north, its deep-blue bay caught within a green amphitheatre of cypresses and olives, the village still reflects the quintessential beauty of old Corfu. Unfortunately, the view from the south includes the modern terraced apartments that dominate the west side of the bay.

The White House, 'set like a dice on a rock already venerable with the scars of wind and water', stands on the south side of the bay. It is distinctly English-looking, with its solid, square shape and its broad, hipped roof. Here Durrell and his wife, Nancy, lived what seems to have been a truly idyllic life in the Ionian sun. Their quickest way to Corfu Town was by boat and they travelled a great deal in their little sailing boat, the *Van Norden*. Their friends were a collection of serene eccentrics. Even the dynamic Henry Miller was persuaded to visit for a time and was captivated by Greece. The fruit of this was Miller's splendid book *The Colossus of Maroussi*. Today, the White House functions as a restaurant with apartments above.

Kalámi has a number of other tavernas, interspersed with villas, the whole softened by groves of orange and lemon trees, olives and cypresses. Although the resort is busy in summer, it is quiet in the evenings. Boats can be rented, and the beach is very safe for children.

✚ 131 D6 ✉ 1km (0.5 miles) off the main coast road, 30km (19 miles) north of Corfu Town 🍴 The White House (€€) 🚌 Green bus from Avramiou Street, Corfu Town–Kassiópi/Loútses. Walk from main road ⛴ Small ferry boats from nearby resorts ❓ Limited parking

6 Kanóni

The resort lies at the southern tip of the Kanóni Peninsula overlooking the two little islands of Vlachérna and Pontikonísi (Mouse Island).

The view of Vlachérna, with its little convent and its solitary cypress tree, and of Pontikonísi, with its thicket of trees and its chapel, is probably the most photographed in the Ionian Islands, an enduring visual symbol of modern Corfu. The sounds accompanying this scenic delight are less soothing: Corfu's airport runway slices across the adjoining lagoon, Chalkiopoúlou, a few hundred metres away. (Youngsters will love plane-spotting.)

There is precedent for sound and fury, however. Kanóni is so named from being the site of a gun battery, first established by the French during the British blockade of Corfu from 1810 to 1815. Today, a Russian cannon, installed about 30 years ago, stands on the viewing terrace overlooking Vlachérna and Pontikonísi. Winding steps lead down from the terrace to the small harbour, from where Vlachérna is reached along a causeway. The Convent of the Virgin Mary here has a fine Venetian belfry. Boats ferry visitors to Pontikonísi and run to and from Corfu Town. The Byzantine Church of Pandokrator on Pontikonísi, is said to date from the 11th or 12th century.

➕ 133 C7 ✉ At the southernmost tip of the Kanóni
Peninsula, 5km (3 miles) south of Corfu Town 🍴 Kanoni
(€–€€) 🚌 2 Kanóni. Blue bus from San Rocco Square
🚢 Caique ferries to and from Corfu Town ❓ Follow parking
signs on approach road and branch right, signed Pontikonísi,
to reach harbourside car park. There is a one-way traffic
system round the tip of the Kanóni Peninsula, so keep a
sharp lookout for the Pontikonísi sign. If you miss it, you
cannot turn back and are left with very limited parking
beside the viewing terrace and café

7

Límni Korissión
(Lake Korissión)

Southwest Corfu is low-lying, a gentle foil to the mountainous north. Typical of the area is Lake Korissión, a large expanse of water that lies on the scimitar curve of the coast behind the remote Halikounas Beach.

Lake Korissión is a man-made lagoon of 607ha (1,500 acres), created by the Venetians, who constructed a short, reinforced channel from the sea and flooded existing marshlands. It offers a peaceful respite from crowded beaches and the more popular resorts. Inland, the lake is bordered by low hills and, to the north, Mount Ágios Matthéos looms large. Even the ever-present olive relents here, to be replaced by silvery-green juniper and cedar trees that lie scattered along the lake shores. Flowering plants at Korissión include the spring catchfly, or loose-flowered orchid, with its purple blooms, just one of the dozen or so orchid species that flourish here. Summer sees the blue-green sea holly and various spurges, and later in the season, the white flowers of the sand lily.

The lake and its margins provide an ideal winter habitat for birds. Over 120 species have been recorded, including rare migrants such as the great white egret and the glossy ibis. Overwintering visitors include mallard, shelduck and teal.

The neck of the channel at the entrance to the lake is blocked with fish traps to control the passage and catching of grey mullet – a rough track runs down the seaward edge of the lake from its northern end to a fish-watcher's hut beside the channel. One of the charms of Lake Korissión is its remoteness, and it has the bonus of a stretch of sandy beach north and south of the channel, although the lake area and adjoining beach can become crowded and noisy at the height of the summer season and on holiday weekends. You can walk south along the beach to escape it all.

✚ 134 C2 ✉ On the west coast about 20km (12.5 miles) south of Corfu Town 🍴 Taverna (€) at north end of lake ❓ The north end of the lake is reached by following signposts for Gardíki from a junction about 1km (0.5 miles) south of Moraïtika. The south end is reached by turning west off the main road to Kávos, at Línia, and following signs for Paralía tou Íssou (Issos Beach)

8 Mouseío Archaiologikó (Archaeological Museum)

Corfu Town's small, but rewarding, Archaeological Museum houses some outstanding relics from the island's ancient past.

The museum contains one of the finest prehistoric relics in all of Greece, the famous Gorgon pediment recovered from the ruins of the 6th-century BC Temple of Artemis on the Kanóni Peninsula. Though it is not intact, the pediment, 17m (56ft) long and 3m (10ft) high, has been restored skilfully. Such monumental antiquity may seem incidental to devoted beach lovers, but the impact of the snake-haired, eye-popping Medusa sheltering her blood offspring, Chrysaor and Pegasus, is enough to excite the most jaded of onlookers, as she looms above, attended by Zeus and slaughtered Titans and flanked by leopards.

The Gorgon frieze is matched, in the South Hall, by the splendid Lion of Menekrates, a limestone sculpture of the late 7th century BC. Discovered in 1843, it is considered to be one of the finest examples of early Corinthian art.

Other delights include some excellent tomb monuments, classical pottery and Bronze Age artefacts, and an impressive collection of coins dating from the 6th to 3rd centuries BC. In the North Hall there are some splendid terracotta fittings and artefacts from the ruins of a 7th-century temple found in the grounds of Mon Repos villa (▶ 52).

The finest exhibit here is the left side of a limestone pediment featuring the god Dionysus and a naked youth, well supplied with wine and reclining on a couch. Both are avidly watching a scene on the lost half of the pediment, a tantalizing omission for the rest of us.

✚ 136 D2 ✉ 5 Vraila Armeni Street ☎ 26610-30680 🕓 Tue–Sun 8.30–3 💷 Moderate. Free on Sun 🍴 Cafés and tavernas in nearby San Rocco Square (€) and on the Liston (€€€) ❓ Photography, without flash, is permitted for some exhibits. Please check with attendants

9 Palaiokastrítsa (Paleokastritsa)

The wooded headlands and crescent-shaped bays of Corfu's most celebrated scenic extravaganza have attracted visitors since the early 19th century.

At Paleokastritsa, towering mountains give way reluctantly to the sea, their tree-clad slopes mottled with great cliffs. Here, the landscape has overwhelmed the human element, instead of the other way round, although in high summer the resort itself is very busy. Roads end at Paleokastritsa, giving a real sense of arrival.

Long before the British holidaymaker first picnicked at 'Paleo', the western headland was home to a **monastery** dedicated to the Virgin Mary. The original foundation was 13th-century, but the present complex is mainly 18th-century. A small church lies at the heart of the monastery, its walls laden with icons in chunky rococo frames; a fine painting of the Last Judgement hangs above the south doorway. From the garden terrace there is a breathtaking view across the Bay of Liapádes to Cape Ágios Iliodoros and on to distant Cape Plaka. Within the monastery complex is a preserved oil mill and a small museum displaying icons, and a collection of shells and bones from the sea.

The less spiritual delights of Paleokastritsa include the rather cramped, sun-trap beaches of Ágios Spyrídon, which lie to either side of the main car park. The harbour and beaches at Alipo Bay lie beyond the easterly headland of St Nicholas. There are sun-loungers and water sports equipment, and boats can be rented from the harbour. Organized boat trips visit nearby cliff grottoes and caves, and the crystal-clear seas round 'Paleo' are especially good for scuba diving.

✚ 128 F4 ✉ On the west coast of Corfu, 25km (15.5 miles) from Corfu Town 🍴 Numerous tavernas and cafés in resort 🚌 Green bus from Avramiou Street, Corfu Town–Paleokastritsa 🚢 Boat trips to view coastal features, caves and grottoes

Monastery
⊙ 8–1, 3–8 💰 A small donation appreciated 🍴 Café-restaurant (€€) outside monastery ❓ Dress appropriately when visiting the monastery

10 Pantokrátoras (Mount Pandokrator)

The mountain's vast bulk, and its rolling hinterland of *maquis* (scrubland) dense with kermes oak, myrtle and wild flowers, creates a persuasive sense of wilderness and open space.

Pandokrator, at 906m (2,971ft) a spectacular viewpoint, was known in prehistory as Istone and by the Venetians as Monte San Salvatore. In the 14th century a church dedicated to Christ Pandocrator, 'The Almighty' or 'The All Embracing One', was built on the summit of the mountain and the name was eventually applied to the entire massif. The present buildings are 19th-century replacements of earlier structures. Today, the monastery shares the crowded summit, rather uneasily, with a huge radio mast and various other beacons and aerials. There is a pilgrimage to the monastery on 6 August each year to celebrate the Feast of the Transfiguration.

From the north the approach is by road, through Néa (New) Períthia (➤ 88) and then by a track to join the summit road. The best approach, however, is from the south through Spartýlas and the village of Strinýlas. Just beyond Strinýlas, bear right at a junction and on to a good road which leads to the summit. The last kilometre, surfaced with ribbed concrete, is extremely tortuous and steep. Parking space at the summit is limited. It may be more practical, and in some ways more fitting, to walk the last section from roadside parking below the summit. Experienced hillwalkers, with proper clothing, footwear and equipment, will find off-road exploration of the mountain rewarding.

➕ 131 C5 ✉ Dominates the northeast corner of the island, 37km (23 miles) north of Corfu Town 🍴 Café outside monastery gate 🖐 Monastery free, small donation welcome ❓ Roadside parking about 1km (0.5 miles) from the summit near the junction with the track from Néa (New) Períthia, signposted Pyrgí, Róda and Kassiópi

Exploring

Corfu has golden sandy beaches, water sports of every kind, choice places to eat and an abundance of nightlife; but there is also a wealth of woodland, mountains and undeveloped coast that provide havens of peace and quiet to explore. The island is steeped in history: in ancient times it was known variously as Scheria and as Drepane, the word for 'sickle', a reference that is thought to derive from the island's long, curved shape. By the medieval period the name Corfu was established. There are several explanations of this name. It is said to derive from the Greek word *koryphai*, meaning 'summit' or 'twin peaks', a possible reference to the two rocky outcrops on which the Old Fortress of Corfu Town is built. Another suggestion is that the Norman invaders of the 12th century named their anchorages north of modern Corfu Town *Corfi*, the Greek plural version of the Latin word for bay, *golfo*.

Kérkyra (Corfu Town)

The original settlement of Corfu Town was on the southern tip of the Kanóni Peninsula to the south of the present town. Then, in the 6th century, a more dangerous world emerged and the town's citizens, exhausted from savage barbarian raids, moved to the small, twin-peaked peninsula where the Old Fortress now stands. Gradually a town developed

outside the fortress, but within its own defensive walls. Later expansion saw Corfu Town spread to the south and west to form an outer shell of suburbs that evolved into the district surrounding San Rocco Square.

The magic of Corfu Town is at its most potent where new and old meet at M Theotoki Square. Here, you step from the bustle of a modern Greek town into the arcaded, smoothly paved streets of medieval times, your way signposted by Greek street names, Greek churches, and by a sense of more variety to come. Soon, you reach the famous Esplanade, its western edge framed by the arcaded Liston. At its northern edge is the Palace of St Michael and St George, symbol of British neoclassicism. Beyond all this, to the east, Byzantine Greece is represented, in spirit, by the Old Fortress, whose Venetian walls stand on Corinthian foundations.

www.gnto.gr ✚ 133 B7

ÁGIOS IÁSONAS KAI SOSIPÁTROS (CHURCH OF ST JASON AND ST SOSIPATER)

Corfu's sole example of 10th- to early 11th-century Byzantine architecture stands in a rather anonymous corner of Anemomylos, a suburb on the southern edge of Corfu Town. Jason and Sosipater were bishops of Tarsus and Iconium respectively, who brought Christianity to Corfu during the first century when the island was under Roman rule. They are said to have been martyred for it. The church is of typical Byzantine design, built in the shape of a cross, with a handsome central dome crowning an octagonal drum. Beams of sunlight passing through the stained glass of the dome create luminous pools of colour. There are a number of fine icons, and a mix of styles and periods. There is an 18th-century iconostasis, and the plain marble columns that help to support the dome are believed to originate from a classical temple of ancient Palaiopolis (▶ 60).

✚ 136 F4 ✉ Iásonas kai Sosipátros (Jason and Sosipater Street) ✋ Free; donations welcome 🍴 Cafés, tavernas (€) in Nafsikas and Dimokratias 🚌 2 Kanóni. Blue bus from San Rocco Square. Get off at Nafsikas Street ↔ Ruined Basilica of Palaiopolis (▶ 60) ❓ Sober clothing should be worn. Ask for key at adjacent house if church is locked

ÁGIOS SPYRÍDONAS

See pages 24–25.

ANAGNOSTIKÍ ETAIRÍA KERKYRAS (CORFU READING SOCIETY)

This venerable society was founded in 1836 by a group of young Corfiot intellectuals, giving it a claim to being the oldest cultural institution in modern Greece. The Society's premises are in a handsome Venetian building at the south end of Arseniou near the Palace of St Michael and St George. Its arcaded façade incorporates an outside staircase and an upper verandah. At street level, a small relief of an owl, symbol of wisdom, strikes a charming and witty note.

The interior of the building has the comfortable, well-worn atmosphere of all good libraries; the walls are hung with paintings and prints.

There is an impressive collection of Ionian-related books, manuscripts, periodicals, engravings, maps and other material by Greek and foreign authors. Researchers and interested visitors are welcomed with great courtesy.

➕ 136 A3 ✉ 120 Kapodistriou Street 🕑 Mon–Sat 9.15–1.45 ✋ Free 🍴 En Plo (€€) 🔀 Palace of St Michael and St George (➤ 61) ❓ The library and the reading room are open to the public

ANGLIKÓ NEKROTAFEÍO (BRITISH CEMETERY)

There is nothing gloomy about a visit to this tree-shaded and flower-filled oasis of peace and quiet. More English garden than burial plot, it was established during the period of the British Protectorate and contains the graves of soldiers who died in service during the 19th and 20th centuries. Civilians are buried here, too.

The cemetery, under the care of the British War Graves Commission, owes much of its charm to the dedication of long-serving caretaker, George Psailas, who was born in the peaceful little guardian house and who, over many years, has tended the cemetery's green spaces with great devotion.

In spring the cemetery is awash with the colour of shrubs and flowers, most notably a remarkable number of orchids, which are allowed to bloom and seed before the grass-cutting begins.

✠ 136 D1 ✉ Kolokotroní (off Mitropolitou Methodiou) ⏱ All day 🍴 Cafés and restaurants (€–€€) in nearby Mitropolitou Methodiou

CAMPIELLO (OLD CORFU TOWN)

See pages 28–29.

DIMOTIKÍ PINAKOTHÍKI (MUNICIPAL ART GALLERY)

This gallery was opened in 1995 in the east wing of the Palace of St Michael and St George (➤ 61). The exhibition rooms are a pleasure in themselves, and the approach, through a tree-shaded garden and past the Art Café and Bar, is charming. The works in the gallery are mainly by 19th- and 20th-century Corfiot painters and sculptors, but there are also medieval paintings including the *Decapitation of John The Baptist* by Michael Damaskinos. Corfiot painters include Charalambos Pachis, whose *The Assassination of Capodistrias* is a touch melodramatic, but compelling. The French-influenced painting of the Liston, *Night in Corfu* (1913), by George Samartzis, has a happy relevance for holidaymakers. Modern works by the engraver Nikolaos Ventouras, and later abstract paintings by Aglaia Papa, are also on display. Next to the café-bar there is another smaller gallery, which stages various exhibitions.

🕀 136 A3 ✉ Paláti tou Agíou Michaíl tou Georgíou (Palace of St Michael and St George, East Wing) ☎ 26610-39553 🕐 Tue–Sat 8.30–3, Sun 9.30–2.30 👆 Moderate 🍴 Art Gallery Café (€€), behind the palace ↔ Palace of St Michael and St George (➤ 61), Old Fortress (➤ 58–59)

KANÓNI

See pages 32–33.

MITRÓPOLI (CATHEDRAL)

Corfu's Orthodox cathedral, the Cathedral of Panagia Spiliotissa (Madonna of the Grotto), stands at the top of a flight of steps set back from the Old Port Square. The 16th-century building, which did not become a cathedral until 1841, is dedicated to St Theodora Augusta, whose mummified remains were brought to Corfu at the same time as those of the more celebrated St Spyrídon. They lie in a silver casket in the cathedral.

The interior of the cathedral is lined with wooden panelling. There is a white iconostasis with a broken pediment, and the numerous icons include a beautiful image of the Archangel Michael and one of the Virgin.

🕀 136 A2 ✉ Plateía Konstantinou, off Old Port Square 🕐 Daily 9–2. Avoid casual visits during services 👆 Free, donations welcome 🍴 Cafés, restaurants (€–€€) in Old Port Square ↔ Old Port Square (➤ 62) ❓ Sober clothing should be worn. Ceremony on first Sunday of Lent when relics of St Theodora are carried around town

MON REPOS

The elegant villa of Mon Repos was built on a choice site on the Kanóni Peninsula in 1831 for the British High Commissioner, Sir Frederick Adam. Its style is neoclassical, with a nod to the Byzantine in its rotunda. The British ceded Mon Repos to King George I

of Greece on their withdrawal from Corfu in 1864. Prince Philip, Duke of Edinburgh, was born here in 1921.

The house had a chequered history in subsequent years and lay neglected as legal disputes dragged on between the former King Constantine of Greece and the Municipality of Corfu. The latter has restored the property, which is now fully open to the public and incorporates the Museum of Palaiópolis. Exhibits include displays on ancient Kérkyra.

At the southern end of the grounds are the impressive ruins of a Doric temple of about 500BC. The only parking available is near the entrance gate and is very limited. An on-site café is planned, but you are advised to bring water with you.

🚼 136 F4 (off map) 📧 Nafsikas, Anemomylos ☎ 26610-41369 🕐 House: Tue–Sun 8.30–3. Park: daily 8.30–7 👆 Grounds free, museum moderate 🍴 Café (€), tavernas (€–€€) in nearby Garítsa 🚌 2 Kanóni. Blue bus from San Rocco Square ↔ Christian Basilica of Palaiopolis (➤ 60)

MOUSEÍO ARCHAIOLOGIKÓ (ARCHAEOLOGICAL MUSEUM)

See pages 36–37.

MOUSEÍO SOLOMOÚ (SOLOMOS MUSEUM)

The poet Dionysios Solomos (1798–1857) was born on the island of Zakynthos but spent his later life on Corfu. He championed the modern Greek language, and in 1863 the first two stanzas of his 1822 poem, 'Hymn to Liberty', were set to music by his friend, the composer Nicholas Mantzaros. The combined work became the Greek national anthem. The museum is a reconstruction of the house in which Solomos lived and which was destroyed during World War II. The atmosphere alone is rewarding.

➕ 136 A2 ✉ 3rd Parados, Arseniou ☎ 26610-30674 🕔 Jun–Oct Mon–Fri 9.30–2; Nov–May Mon–Fri 9.30–1 💰 Moderate 🍴 Cafés, restaurants (€–€€) in Old Port Square ↔ Byzantine Museum (► 54) ❓ Labels in Greek only. No photography

MOUSEÍO VIZANTINÓ (BYZANTINE MUSEUM)

The Church of Panagia Antivouniotissa (Church of the Blessed Virgin), which houses this outstanding collection of Byzantine art, dates from the 16th century. There are about 90 icons on display, most from the 13th to the 17th centuries and depicting individual saints and biblical scenes. There is also outstanding work by the Cretan painters Emanuel Tzanes and Michael Damaskinos, among others. The plain outside walls of the church mask a beautiful interior of enclosed arcades surrounding a central nave with a coffered and decorated ceiling, painted walls and gilded woodwork.

🚹 136 A3 ✉ Arseniou (Mourayia) ☎ 26610-38313 ⏰ Tue–Sun 8.30–3 ✋ Moderate 🍴 Cafés, restaurants (€–€€) in Old Port Square, Faliraki (€€) ↔ Solomos Museum (➤ 52–53) ❓ Exhibits generally in English and Greek. No flash photography

NÉO FROÚRIO (NEW FORTRESS)

The New Fortress is 'new' only in the sense that it was started in 1572, a mere 15 years after the Venetians began rebuilding the Old Fortress. The massive outerworks of this 'Néo Froúrio' were built by the Venetians, but the buildings that survive within the walls, a mass of tunnels, vaulted chambers and stairways, were added by the British. On its eastern side are two entrances: an unused one in Solomou Square; the other, in New Fortress Square, is the military gate, used by the resident naval authorities. Public entrance is via the steep stone steps that lead up from the far end of the square past the Roman Catholic Church of Tenedos. There are fine views from the bastions and at the top a café/bar, exhibition centre and museum of ceramics (not always open).

🚹 136 A1 ✉ Solomos Street, off Spilia Square or New Fortress Square ☎ 26610-27477 ⏰ May–Oct daily 9–9 ✋ Moderate 🍴 Café (€), tavernas (€–€€) in nearby Old Port Square ↔ Old Port (➤ 62)

a walk into the past

A walk through the historic southern part of Corfu Town.

Start at the Peristýlio Maitland (Maitland Rotunda, ➤ 70). Continue south on Dimokratias, alongside the sea, to the small harbour at Anemomylos. Here, on the seaward point, beyond the Nautilus Café, is a restored windmill. Pass the café and bear right along the edge of the sea until opposite Hotel Mon Repos. Cross the road, with care, then go down the lane to the left of the hotel. Pass Ágios Iásonas kai Sosipátros (the Church of St Jason and St Sosipater, ➤ 46–47) on the left.

Turn first right just past the church. Reach a tree-shaded walkway (toilets) and turn left. At a road junction cross

left, with care, and follow the continuation walkway to reach Oveliskos Ntalklas (the Douglas Obelisk). Cross left to the British Consulate.

The obelisk commemorates General Sir Howard Douglas, the 4th British High Commissioner, an able administrator.

Go up the street to the left of the consulate. At a junction go straight across and past railings to reach Stili tou Menekráti (the Tomb of Menekrates).

This 6th-century cenotaph celebrates Menekrates, a representative of ancient Corcyra.

Continue along Kyprou (Cyprus) Street for about 100m (110yds), then make a sharp U-turn to the right on to a road rising through trees. Continue until you reach a T-junction by the walls of Corfu Prison. Turn left and follow the walls round past the prison's main gate. Bear left, and then right down Kolokotroni Street to Anglikó Nekrotafeío (the British Cemetery, ➤ 48–49). Continue on to a busy junction with Mitropolitou Methodiou. Turn right and then continue to San Rocco Square.

Distance 5km (3 miles)
Time 1.5 hours
Start point Maitland Rotunda
End point San Rocco Square
Lunch Cafés and tavernas ✉ Mitr Athanassiou (€)

NÉO LIMANI (NEW PORT)

The area of the New Port is neither scenic nor tourist-oriented, but it is a lively place, full of everyday activities and the rattle and hum of seagoing vessels. Boats, large and small, throng the working harbour, while the big mainland and island ferries come and go along the quays further north. The busy seafront road is lined with ships' chandlers, marine suppliers and workshops, as well as travel agencies and car-rental firms. At the western end is the old and down-to-earth district of Mandouki, with its cafés and tavernas.

✚ 136 A1 (off map) ✉ Ethnikis Antistasseos ✋ Free 🍴 Cafés, tavernas (€–€€) in nearby Mandouki 🚢 Main port for big ferries ⟷ Monastery of the Virgin (➤ 69), Old Port (➤ 62)

PALAIÓ FROÚRIO (OLD FORTRESS)

The Palaió Froúrio (Paleo Froúrio) is a powerful visual symbol of town and island. The earliest known fortifications were Byzantine, established in the 6th century after the destruction of the old Corinthian city of Palaiopolis (➤ 60) by Goth raiders. The Venetians replaced and extended the walls in the 15th century and excavated the defensive moat, the Contrafossa, that now adds such a picturesque element to the scene. Further rebuilding took place between 1558 and 1588, and it is these fortifications that survive today.

The fortress is approached from the east side of the Esplanade. The right-hand guardhouse in the main gatehouse houses the Byzantine Collection of Corfu with mosaics and sculptures from the Basilica of Palaiopolis. There are fresco fragments from St Nicholas's church in Kato Korakiana. Across the bridge is the Church of the Madonna of the Carmelites. The summit of the inner peak, the Castel a Terra (Landward Castle), with its little lighthouse, can be reached by a steep climb past a Venetian clock-tower. At 72m (236ft) high, the view over Corfu Town and inland to Mount Pandokrator (➤ 40–41) is spectacular.

There is a maze of tunnels, excavated by the Venetians, beneath the Old Fortress and the New Fortress. One tunnel is said to run beneath the sea to Vídos Island, which lies just offshore from the town. Vídos was strategically important to both attack on the town and, when fortified, to its defence.

✚ 136 B4 ✉ Spianáda (Esplanade) ☎ 26610-48310 ◐ May–Oct daily 8.30–7; Nov–Apr daily 8.30–3 ✋ Expensive ⬛ Café (€€) ↔ Municipal Art Gallery (➤ 50–51), Palace of St Michael and St George (➤ 61), Esplanade (➤ 70)

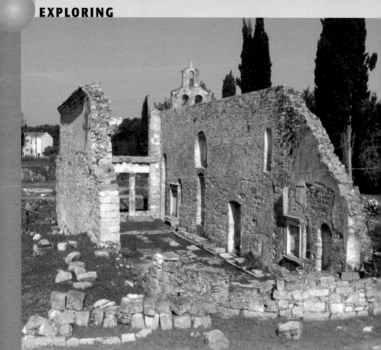

PALAIOPOLIS (ANCIENT CITY OF CORCYRA)

Poignant relics of Palaiopolis (Paleopolis), the ancient city of
Corcyra, survive on the Kanóni Peninsula 5km (3 miles) south of
Corfu Town. One of the oldest ruins is the Tower of Nerandzicha, a
remnant of the city walls dating from the 5th century BC. Close by
are the impressive remains of the late 6th-century BC Temple of
Artemis, from which the Gorgon pediment, now housed in Corfu
Town's Archaeological Museum (➤ 36–37), was recovered.

On the road to Kanóni, opposite the gates to Mon Repos
(➤ 52), are the ruins of the 5th-century Christian Basilica of
Palaiopolis. Nearby are the ruins of Roman baths of about AD200.

✚ 136 F4 (off map) or 133 C7 ⊠ Anemomylos 🖐 Free 🍴 Cafés, tavernas
(€–€€) in nearby Garitsa 🚌 2 Kanóni. Blue bus from San Rocco Square
↔ Mon Repos (➤ 52)

PALÁTI TOU AGÍOU MICHAÍL TOU GEORGÍOU
(PALACE OF ST MICHAEL AND ST GEORGE)

Dominating the Plateía, the northern end of the Esplanade, the palace is the most striking relic of the 50-year British presence on Corfu. It was built between 1819 and 1824 during the service of Sir Thomas Maitland, the first High Commissioner, and was used as the official seat of the Protectorate. The palace is triumphantly neoclassical in style, with a passing nod to the Parthenon in its Doric portico. In the garden in front of the palace stands a statue of Sir Frederick Adam, second High Commissioner.

The interior is outstanding: the finest feature is the rotunda on the first floor, its domed ceiling painted in blue and gold, its walls punctuated with mahogany doors, niches and mirrored panels.

Several of the state rooms house the Museum of Asiatic Art, a remarkable collection of Sino-Japanese art and artefacts, including mosaics from the early Christian Basilica of Palaiopolis (opposite).

Chinese and Japanese exhibits make up the largest part of the collection but there are also objects from India, Tibet, Nepal, Korea and Thailand. Items include prehistoric bronzes, porcelain ware, woodcarvings, Noh theatre masks, Samurai armour and weapons and much more. The palace also houses the Municipal Art Gallery (➤ 50–51) and the Modern Art Museum.

✚ 136 A3 ✉ Spianáda (Esplanade) ☎ 26610-30443

🕐 Tue–Sun 8.30–3 👍 Moderate 🍴 Art Gallery Café (€€) ➡ New Fortress (➤ 54), Old Fortress (➤ 58–59), Esplanade (➤ 70)

PALÉO LIMANI (OLD PORT)

There is an unassuming charm about the Old Port which reflects its historic role as a maritime and commercial centre. Old Port Square was once used for the town market, and local people still gather here to gossip and relax. The quays are used for car parking, but the inner square has been landscaped and is lined with some fine old buildings, including the Law Courts and the Constantinople Hotel. Lanes and alleyways lead temptingly into the old town from here.

Behind the Law Courts is a splendid medieval relic, the gate of the Venetian Granary, complete with a stone relief of the trireme, or rowing galley – the emblem of Old Corfu. The right-hand side of Old Port Square leads into Solomou Square and then into Spilia Square, or New Fortress Square, and so to the New Fortress; the district is still called Ovriaki from its time as the Jewish Quarter.

There are a number of cafés and tavernas in Old Port Square. From the square, Donzelot Street leads up to the area known as the Mourayia and into Arseniou Street. Here, you can see Venetian buildings, as well as the Solomos Museum and the Byzantine Museum.

✚ 136 A2 ✉ Spilia 🍴 Cafés, tavernas (€–€€) 🖐 Free 🚢 Ferry port for Paxos and excursions ↔ Cathedral of Panagia Spiliotissa (➤ 51), New Fortress (➤ 54), Solomos Museum (➤ 52–53), Byzantine Museum (➤ 54)

PLATEÍA AGÍOU SPYRÍDONA (ST SPYRÍDON'S SQUARE)

This attractive Italianate square lies at the heart of Corfu Town. Its official name is Plateía Iroon Kypriakou Agonos, the Square of the Heroes of the Cypriot Struggle, but the nearby Church of St Spyrídon has given it the more manageable name of St Spyrídon's Square, or the Saint's Square. Two other churches stand nearby. The Church of the Virgin of Strangers, which dates from the 1680s, became the favoured church of exiled Greeks from mainland Epirus fleeing from their Turkish oppressors. The interior of the church is particularly rich in icons and frescoes. The other church is that of St John the Baptist, or St John at the Cisterns, named after the rainwater tanks that once lay beneath the square. On the western side of the square is the handsome classical façade of the 19th-century Ionian Bank.

✚ 136 B3 🍴 Café Plakada (€€) ⟷ Church of St Spyrídon (► 24–25)

an excursion to Paxoí and Antipaxoí

PAXOÍ (PAXOS)

Paxoí (Paxos) lies 48km (30 miles) to the south of Corfu Town, just 11km (7 miles) south of Ákrotírio Asprókavos, and is a popular destination for day excursions from Corfu. It is decidedly up-market, thanks to the large number of visiting yacht crews and to Paxos devotees with a proprietorial air. Prices tend to be above the average for the Ionian as a whole, due in part to the high cost of imports.

The island, 11km (7 miles) long and 5km (3 miles) wide, is swathed in olive trees, pines and cypresses, giving the hilly interior a deceptively rounded look. It is a delightful place, where life is measured at a much slower pace than on Corfu. Dusty tracks wind through the olive groves to small settlements or to remote coves and pebble beaches – although Paxos is not a beach-lover's paradise.

The south and west coasts are particularly spectacular, with steep cliffs, huge, cathedral-like sea caves and wind-sculpted rock formations, such as the stupendous pinnacle of Tripitos, linked by an arch to the south coast. The limestone of the cliffs glows pink and ochre in the setting sun.

The Venetians oversaw the 15th-century transformation of Paxos into one enormous olive grove, and the Paxíots created an almost formal landscape of terraces and drystone walling that survives today. The Venetian influence is seen also in the buildings of the island's principal port, Gáïos, and in tiny hamlets and numerous scattered ruins. Offshore from Gáïos is the tree-covered island of St Nicholas, complete with its ruins of a 15th-century Venetian fortress. The smaller Panagia Islet has an old church and a lighthouse.

The two other main settlements are Lákka at the northern tip of the island, and Longós, on the east coast, midway between Gáïos and Lákka. Buses operate between all three, but exploring the island on foot is a rewarding option, although you need more than a day visit to get the best from this Ionian jewel.

ANTÍPAXOÍ (ANTIPAXOS)

Antipaxos is only a few kilometres from Paxos and can be reached from Gáïos by fast ferry boat. A mere 3sq km (1sq mile) in size, the island is a complex of tracks and paths through olive- and vine-growing country, a place where some kind of solitude can be found even at the height of summer. The east-coast beaches at Vrika, Mesovrika and Voutoumi are attractive, although they tend to become crowded with day visitors.

Getting there

Ferries operate to Paxos from Corfu Town and there are cruise boats from Kávos. It is essential to make enquiries at several ferry agencies because of a complex and often changing ferry system. There is a seaplane service run by AirSea Lines that operates between Gouviá, Corfu and Paxos (▶ 12 and 14).

PLATEÍA DEMARCHÍOU (TOWN HALL SQUARE)

Known officially as Plateía Demarchíou, this attractive central square, where there are several craft shops and pâtisseries, descends in a series of paved terraces from south to north. At the centre stands a bust of Iakovos Polylas (1825–93), friend of the poet Dionysios Solomos, and himself a distinguished writer and translator. Guilford Street, named after Frederick North, fifth Earl of Guilford, leads into the square. Guilford was a genial eccentric and enthusiastic Grecophile, who converted to Greek Orthodoxy and brought to fruition John Capodistrias's dream of an Ionian Academy, the first university in modern Greece. Count John Capodistrias (Ioannis Kapodistrias; 1776–1831) was a celebrated Corfiot who, in 1827, became the first President of Independent Greece. In 1831 his career was cut short when he was assassinated at Náfplio in the Peloponnese by critics of his political programme. Born in Corfu in 1776, Capodistrias practised as a doctor, and then entered island politics. During the French occupation of Corfu he left the island and joined the Russian foreign service. In 1822 he retired and devoted himself to the cause of Greek independence. Capodistrias is buried in Moní Platytéras (the Monastery of Platitéra) in Corfu Town. A small museum in Evropoúli, to the west of the town, celebrates his life.

The focus of the square is Corfu Town Hall, an intriguing building that has undergone a number of transformations since its origins in the late 17th century as an open arcade, the Loggia dei Nobili, a meeting place of the Venetian hierarchy. It was subsequently converted to a theatre, and a second floor was added when it became the Town Hall in

1903. On the east wall is a spectacular marble relief depicting
Francesco Morosini – Venetian Admiral (later Doge of Venice),
Hammer of the Turks in the Peloponnese, and incidental
demolisher of the Athenian Parthenon when he bombarded the
Turkish-held Acropolis in 1687 (the Parthenon was the Turk's
gunpowder store). Morosini glares threateningly at the
handsome façade of the Roman Catholic Cathedral of St James
and St Christopher diagonally opposite. The original St James's
was a parish church of 1588 and became a cathedral in 1633.
After much damage from bombing in 1943, the present building
was restored.

✚ 136 B3 ♿ Free 🍴 Bougainvillea (€–€€)

PLATEÍA G THEOTÓKI IOÁNNOU
(SAN ROCCO SQUARE)

Corfu Town's commercial heart is as brash and traffic-bound as central Athens. But it does have a heart. The central plaza has seating, though a pause for quiet reflection is not an option, and busy shopping streets radiate from all corners. There are numerous hot-food shops and several street kiosks along the north side. The Blue Bus terminus is on the southeast side. Polihroni Konstanda Street leads off the west corner of San Rocco and, though heavy with traffic, is worth exploring for its arcaded walkways and food shops. Mitropolitou Methodiou Street leads southwest, and the attractive Alexandras Avenue, with a number of pavement cafés, leads southeast. G Theotoki Street leads northeast into the old town past some wonderful shops, especially on its south side. Do not miss the morning market, reached up Gerasimou Markora Street on the north side of San Rocco Square.

✠ 136 C2 🍴 Cafés, restaurant (€–€€)

PLATITÉRA (MONASTERY OF THE VIRGIN)

Platitéra, meaning 'Wider than the Heavens', is an oasis of calm alongside Corfu Town's busy link road to the coast road north: traffic hurtles past the palm-filled little entrance courtyard and its tall, red-domed bell-tower. Although the original 18th-century convent was set on fire by the French in 1798 in response to a revolt against them by local people, it was soon rebuilt. There are very fine icons and paintings inside the church, although the poor light does not do them justice. The most dramatic are The *Day of Judgement*, by the 16th-century Cretan painter George Klotzas, and the *Allegory of Heavenly Jerusalem*, or, more pointedly, *The Damned and the Blessed*, by an unknown 16th-century artist. The latter brims with graphic symbols of wickedness. Behind the sanctuary is the tomb of Count John Capodistrias.

✠ 136 C1 (off map) ✉ Andreadi
🕐 Daily 9–2 ✋ Free, but donations welcomed 🍴 Cafés, tavernas (€–€€) in nearby Mandouki ⟷ New Port (➤ 58)
❓ Sober clothing should be worn

THE SPIANÁDA (ESPLANADE) AND THE LISTON

Corfu Town's Esplanade is one of the most charming urban open spaces in the Mediterranean. It owes its open nature to the Venetians, who cleared the medieval town that lay in front of the fortress. They ensured that the line of their buildings along the western edge incorporated straight alleyways to allow direct lines of fire from the Old Fortress. These buildings survive along Kapodistriou Street, but on the Plateía, the northern section of the Esplanade, the terrace of arcaded buildings known as the Liston was built by the French in the style of the Parisian rue de Rivoli. Today, with its stylish cafés and restaurants, the Liston is a focus for Corfu Town at play. In front of the Liston is the wide green space used for cricket matches.

The southern half of the Esplanade is landscaped and has an elegant bandstand where the town's brass bands perform on summer Sunday afternoons. At its far end is the Peristýlio Maitland (Maitland Rotunda), built in honour of Sir Thomas Maitland, the first High Commissioner during the early years of the British Protectorate.

✚ 136 B3 🎟 Free 🍴 Café/restaurants (€€–€€€) on the Liston ↔ Palace of St Michael and St George (▶ 61), Old Fortress (▶ 58–59)

Northern Corfu

**Northern Corfu offers
the full range of the
island's charms: beach
resorts, hill villages,
wetlands and the mighty
Mount Pandokrator,
whose wilder reaches
provide an escape from the
crowds and whose rocky eastern
slopes drop steeply to quiet coves and
dazzling shingle beaches.**

North-coast resorts have developed rapidly to keep
pace with the many holidaymakers who flock to the area and the
busy coast roads are lined with bars, cafés, tavernas, shops and
clubs, but it's still possible to find a flavour of an older Corfu
tucked away in the back
streets of many villages
and resorts.

To experience the
essence of Corfu you
need to plan. A rental car
gives independence, but
responsibility. A stress-
free alternative is the rural
bus service. Walking can
be combined with bus
connections to get even
closer to traditional Corfu:
some of the best walking
areas are on the more
remote northeast coast,
and the mountain trails of
Mount Pandokrator.

ACHARÁVI
(AHARAVI)

A popular family resort on Corfu's north coast, Acharávi lies a short distance inland from the beach and to either side of the wide main road. The wooded heights of Mount Pandokrator rise impressively behind and a different world of dense olive groves and quiet villages, such as Epískepsi and Láfki, can be quickly, if steeply, reached from the resort.

Acharávi has a range of shops and eating places. Villas and hotels fill the space between village and seafront. The sand and shingle beach shelves gently and bathing is safe. Water sports are available here, and there are beachside cafés and tavernas. The remote Paralía Almyroú (Almirós Beach) lies at the east end of Acharávi's long strand. This is less crowded but the shoreline has low mudstone reefs, which children may find awkward and slippery.

✚ 130 B3 ✉ 38km (23 miles) north of Corfu Town, on north coast main road 🍴 Beachside tavernas and cafés (€–€€) 🚌 Green bus from Avramiou Street, Corfu Town–Acharávi ❓ Limited parking on beachfront

ÁGIOS SPYRÍDON
(ÁGIOS SPYRÍDONAS)

Standing on a small, peaceful bay at the northeast corner of Corfu, opposite the mountainous coast of Albania, Ágios Spyrídon is reached from the main road down a lane twisting through olive groves. At one time this appealing area was relatively free of buildings, but there has been increasing development, including construction of a big hotel complex. There is a little crescent-shaped beach of fine sand. Behind lies the important wetland area of the Andinioti Lagoon, a protected wildlife site that nurtures a host of birds, insects, mammals and wild flowers. A bridge spans the lagoon outlet and leads on to Ákrotírio (Cape) Agías Aikaterínis, which is worth exploring.

Just inland from the cape, amid pine trees, is the old monastery of Agia Ekaterini (St Katherine). A track leads, in about 3km (2 miles), to Paralía Almyroú (Almirós Beach).

✚ 130 A4 ✉ On north coast 43km (27 miles) from Corfu Town ⅋ Tavernas at Ágios Spyrídon and at Almirós (€–€€) ❓ Limited roadside parking

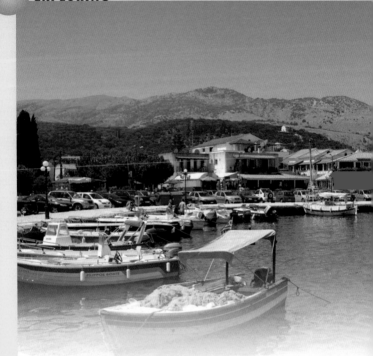

ÁGIOS STÉFANOS (NORTHEAST)

The fishing village of Ágios Stéfanos has kept its traditional character while adapting gracefully to its other role as a resort. Set within the arms of a quiet bay, it is reached down a road which winds through olive groves, then descends through steep bends to the coast. Early and late in the day, it feels as if the way of life that has flourished here for generations has hardly changed at all. To the east, across the narrow waters of the Corfu Channel, lies Albania, here at its closest point to Corfu. The beaches become crowded in summer when excursion boats bring day visitors from nearby Kassiópi and Kalámi. Boats and beach equipment can be rented, and some water sports are available.

Tracks and paths lead north to the isolated beach at Avláki (➤ 80). The road south ends at the very long beach of Kerasiá.

Although this is an undeveloped area – apart from a single taverna and some villas – Paralía Kerasiás (Kerasiá Beach) is very popular with day visitors, who arrive in large numbers by excursion boat.

✚ 137 C7 ✉ 35km (22 miles) north of Corfu Town on the northeast coast. A 3km (2-mile) lane leads to the village from Siniés on the main coast road 🍴 Several tavernas (€€) 🚌 Green bus from Avramiou Street, Corfu Town–Siniés, then walk ⛴ Ágios Spyrídon and Kerasiá can both be reached from Kassiópi and other resorts by boat ❓ Limited parking

AGNI

Agni lies on the tree-shrouded northeast coast of Corfu to the south of Kalámi. A narrow lane leads for over 1km (0.5 miles) down a steep-sided valley from the main road just before Kéntroma village, but driving is not advised and it is wiser to walk down to the small beach. Agni is often reached by boat from neighbouring resorts. The tavernas here are noted for their good food, and they are popular and often busy. It is possible to walk along the coast from Agni, north to Kalámi, or south to Nissaki, passing the old chapel of St Arsenious on the way.

✚ 131 D6 ✉ 28km (17 miles) north of Corfu Town on northeast coast 🍴 Taverna Agni (€€) 🚌 Green bus from Avramiou Street, Corfu Town–Kassiópi to main road turn-off, then 1km (0.5 miles) walk ⛴ Caiques from Kalámi and from resorts to the south ❓ Parking is very difficult

around northeast Corfu

a drive

This is a route of dramatic contrasts, following Corfu's scenic northeast coast and returning through the mountains.

Start at the Old Port in Corfu Town. Drive west from Old Port along Xenofondos Stratigou and Eth Antistasseos. Continue along the coast road for 3km (2 miles) to a big junction. Go right, and after 10km (6 miles), at Tzavros, turn off right, signposted Dassiá. Pass through Dassiá (➤ 82–83), Ipsos (➤ 92) and Barmpáti (➤ 80). Pass through Nissaki (➤ 88) and 5km (3 miles) further on reach the turn off for Kalámi (➤ 30–31).

Parking is limited at Kalámi, but there is a large lay-by on the main road just before the turn off. From here it's under 1km (0.5 miles) to Kalámi and Kouloúra (➤ 87).

Continue along the main road to Kassiópi (➤ 84–85) and on to Acharávi (➤ 72). Halfway through Acharávi's wide main street, pass a walled roundabout with an old waterpump at its centre. About 150m (165yds) further on, look out for a signpost pointing left to Epískepsi and Ágios Panteleímon. Turn left on to a narrow road. Continue steeply and through many bends (watch for occasional pot-holes). In 5km (3 miles), reach Epískepsi.

Epískepsi is a traditional mountain village at the heart of olive-growing country.

Continue for 9km (5.5 miles) to Sgourádes. (Watch out for children on narrow bends through the village.) After 10km (6 miles) reach a junction with a road going off left, signposted Petáleia and Strinýlas (Strinilas). This leads to Mount Pandokrator. Divert if desired. On the main route, continue downhill to Spartýlas. In the 4km (2.5-mile) descent to the coast road there are 25 hair-raising hairpins with stunning views: concentrate. At the coast road, turn right and return to Corfu Town through Ipsos.

Distance 80km (50 miles); 100km (62 miles) if Mount Pandokrator is included
Time 6 hours, with stops; 7–8 hours if Mount Pandokrator is included
Start/end point Corfu Town ✚ 133 B7
Lunch The Pump House (€–€€) ✉ Acharavi
☎ 26630-63271

ÁKROTÍRIO KOMMÉNO
(CAPE KOMMÉNO)

The wooded promontory of Cape Komméno
encloses a small south-facing bay at the
northern end of the larger Gouviá Bay. The
resort's hotels and villas are at the top end of
the price range.

Komméno has its own version of Kanóni's
little church at Vlachérna (➤ 32) in the form of
the church at Ypapanti on its causeway
island. Several manufactured beaches lie along
the wooded shores, but they are small and
monopolized by hotel guests.

In 1537 and again in 1716, Turkish armies
landed in the Cape Komméno and Gouviá area
in ultimately unsuccessful bids to capture
Venetian Corfu.

➕ 130 F4 ✉ 11km (7 miles) north of Corfu Town.
Reached from coast road north of Gouviá just after
branching right from the road to Paleokastritsa 🍴 There
are a number of good-quality restaurants (€€–€€€)
❓ Limited parking

ÁNO KORAKIÁNA

Áno, or Upper, Korakiána is a handsome hill
village with a strong Venetian element to its
buildings and its churches; it even has its own
Philharmonic Society.

The village lies along the tree-covered foothills
of the western massif of Mount Pandokrator
(➤ 40–41). The Church of St Athanasios has
an 18th-century fresco of St Spyrídon and St
Athanasios banishing a dragon, the symbol of a
4th-century plague. At the village's midpoint is

the façade of a house displaying
the less spiritual but highly
diverting sculptures of local
'popular' artist Arestides Zach
Metallinos.

The road north from here
zigzags madly up the curtain wall
of the mountain to Sokráki and
on to the aptly named Zygós
(Zigós), perched on the mountain
slopes and taking its name from
zigaria, meaning 'balance'.

✚ 130 E2 ✉ 18km (11 miles)
northwest of Corfu Town 🍴 Cafés in
village (€) 🚌 Green bus from
Avramiou Street, Corfu Town–
Korakiána ❓ Small car park

AVLÁKI

Avláki comes as something of a surprise because of its refreshing lack of development, although it can become quite busy when day visitors arrive by excursion boat. A narrow road leads from the main road past the holiday complex of Village Michael Angelo, then winds down to the coast through olive groves and open country for just over 1km (0.5 miles). A long swathe of shingle and sand skirts the shores of a deep bay and dense olive groves cover the slopes behind. There are some villas among the trees, plus a couple of tavernas. A windsurfing and dinghy sailing centre is based here. Kassiópi and Ágios Stéfanos are reached by paths and tracks along the coast to north and south.

➕ 131 B7 ✉ 35km (22 miles) north of Corfu Town. Turn off main coast road just before Kassiópi 🍴 Cavo Barbaro Taverna; Avláki Taverna (€–€€) 🚌 Day trips from Kassiópi (➤ 84–85) ❓ Parking behind beach and at south end

BARMPÁTI (BARBATI)

At Barbati the steep slopes of Mount Pandokrator crowd the shoreline. Behind the beach and the main road the rocky flanks of the mountain rise from dense olive groves. Barbati has a long, silvery-white, shingle beach, ideal for youngsters because it offers safe and sheltered bathing, and lies far enough below the road to escape traffic noise. Water sports include waterskiing, windsurfing and parascending, with pedaloes and dinghies for the less adventurous. The village has supermarkets, gift shops and tavernas. Nightlife is limited to quiet drinks and meals; the only thing missing on this eastern shore is a view of the sunset.

➕ 130 E4 ✉ 20km (12.5 miles) north of Corfu Town. Beach is down slip road at south entrance to resort 🍴 Tavernas and cafés (€–€€) 🚌 Green bus from Avramiou Street, Corfu Town–Kassiópi ❓ Limited parking on main road

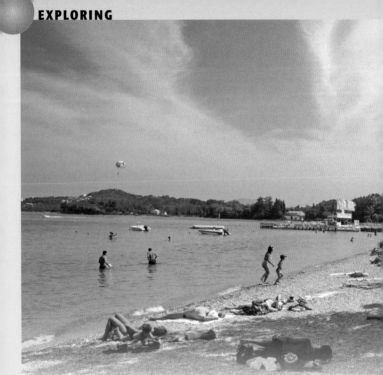

DASSIÁ (DASIÁ)

Dassiá's shingle beach is spared the roadside clamour of other resorts, but its popularity and proximity to Corfu Town makes the seafront a busy place. A zone of hotels and apartments lies between the beach and the main road which has the bulk of gift shops, tavernas and services, as well as the frontages of two big hotels, the Corfu Chandris and the Dasiá Chandris. There is a popular campsite inland from the main road. The beach's shallow waters, reached down narrow lanes, make it safe for young children. Wooden jetties run seaward to cater for the boats that arrive loaded with day visitors or leave for trips. Water sports, including waterskiing and paragliding, add to the bustle, and there are beachfront café-bars and tavernas. The resort of Dafnilia at the southern end of the bay is now merged with Dassiá. About 1km

(0.5 miles) inland is Káto Korakiána, worth a visit for the Greek National Gallery Annexe of Corfu, known also as the Castello Art Gallery.

 130 F4 ⊠ 13km (8 miles) north of Corfu Town on main road 🍴 Choice of cafés, snack bars on beach (€–€€) 🚌 Blue bus No 7 from San Rocco Square, Corfu Town–Dassiá 🛥 Excursions from beach ❓ Roadside parking

GOUVIÁ

Gouviá (close to Corfu Town and therefore popular) lies on the shores of a deep bay between the horned promontories of Ákrotírio Komméno and Ákrotírio Tourka. Kondókali (► 86) lies at the southern end of the bay. Dominating part of the southern shoreline is the Gouviá yacht marina, which has increased the general activity at both resorts. The narrow shingle beach at Gouviá becomes crowded in summer, especially since ferries from Corfu Town bring in large numbers of day visitors. There is enough beach equipment and water sports, including paragliding, to suit all tastes, and bathing is very safe. The resort has numerous restaurants, tavernas, cafés, bars and shops, with the nightlife geared towards young people.

Gouviá Bay was used by the Venetians as a harbour and as a ship-repair and provisioning station.

🚏 133 A5 ⊠ 8km (5 miles) north of Corfu Town 🍴 Snack bars and tavernas (€–€€) 🚌 Blue bus 7 from San Rocco Square, Corfu Town–Kondókali–Gouviá–Dassiá 🛥 Excursion boats from Corfu Town ❓ Parking at south end of beach near marina

KALÁMI

See pages 30–31.

KASSIÓPI

The old port of Kassiópi lies within a picturesque setting of wooded promontories. Today the village is a thriving resort but mixed in are relics of its ancient past. There was a prehistoric settlement here and a Corinthian 'city' long before the Romans colonized the site. Beneath the village church lie the remains of a temple to Jupiter Cassius, from whom Kassiópi gets its name. Wealthy Romans came here for recreation, including Cato, Cicero and Tiberius. The Romans fortified the headland above the harbour, and a castle was built in the 13th century by the Angevin rulers of Corfu. The Venetians wrecked this fortress and built one of their own, the broken walls of which still encircle the crown of the hill. Kassiópi's church is dedicated to the Blessed Virgin Kassiópitra, and possesses an icon of the Virgin that was credited at one time with having miraculous powers. This made the village a place of pilgrimage long before Spyrídon became Corfu's patron saint.

Kassiópi is a working fishing port and the harbour has a lively atmosphere. The pebble beaches are small and hidden away behind headlands.

✚ 131 B6 ✉ 37km (23 miles) north of Corfu Town on main coast road 🍴 Large choice of snack bars and tavernas (€–€€) 🚌 Green bus from Avramiou Street, Corfu Town–Kassiópi 🚢 Ferry boats to and from Corfu Town. Excursions to other resorts ❓ Very limited parking at the harbour and at the north end of the resort by Kalamionas Beach

KÉNTROMA (KÉNDROMA)

On the northeast coast between the better known resorts of Nissaki and Kalámi are a number of tiny coves with shingle beaches; they are reached down steep, narrow lanes, which are unsuitable for cars, branching off from the main road. Kéndroma lies just to the south of Agni (➤ 75) amid a coastal landscape of tree-covered slopes ending at rocky promontories and a sea of exquisite blues and greens.

A short distance southwest of Kéndroma is the Sol Elite Nisáki Beach Hotel, beyond which is Kamináki, another tiny cove with nothing but a shingle beach and a nearby taverna.

✚ 131 D6 ✉ 28km (17 miles) north of Corfu Town on northeast coast
🍴 Tavernas (€) at coves 🚌 Green bus from Avramiou Street, Corfu Town–Kassiópi to main road turn-off, then 0.5km (0.3-mile) walk 🚢 Excursion boats visit ❓ Parking and turning at the beaches can be extremely difficult

KONTÓKALI (KONDÓKALI)

Kondókali, the first resort to the north of Corfu Town, is fast becoming the service centre for the expanding marina that takes up the adjoining shoreline. The resort has an excellent range of restaurants, tavernas and bars. The narrow pebble beaches become crowded in summer. Extended and modernized, the marina has capacity for over 800 boats and is now equipped with most services and facilities, including car rental. It is the island's main base for yacht chartering. The bay on which Kondókali and its neighbour Gouviá stand was once used by the Venetians as a harbour and service port. At the northern end of the resort a lane, signposted 'Venetian Boatyard', leads to the shore and then turns left alongside the marina's perimeter fence. At the road end are the remains of a Venetian 'arsenal' or boat-repair yard, a striking collection of skeletal arches with faded Venetian motifs.

✚ 133 A5 ✉ 7km (4 miles) north of Corfu Town 🍴 Restaurants and snack bars (€–€€) 🚌 Blue bus No 7, from San Rocco Square, Corfu Town–Kondókali–Gouviá–Dassiá 🅿 Limited roadside parking

KOULOÚRA

Kouloúra is a close neighbour to Kalámi, but has a rare sense of exclusiveness, partly because there is no beach to speak of. Excursion boats visit Kouloúra, whose name derives from the Greek word for 'ring shape' or 'lifebuoy' because of the encircling shape of the tiny bay that is set against a backdrop of cypresses and pines. Its charm is enhanced by the curve of a harbour breakwater that shelters fishing boats, and by a handsome house that stands on the site of an ancient fortress and that retains the bell-tower of a medieval chapel. The house is private; its outlook is to the sea, its privacy secured by trees. On calm days, the Corfu Channel between here and Albania can seem like an inland lake. There is a very popular restaurant within the complex.

➕ 131 D7 ✉ 31km (19 miles) north of Corfu Town 🍴 Restaurant. Also tavernas at Kalami (€€) 🚢 Excursion boats visit ❓ Very limited parking at Kouloúra; turning is awkward

NISÁKI (NISSAKI)

The coastline here, below Mount Pandokrator's steep slopes, consists of a series of tiny, rocky coves. Cafés and tavernas on the twisting main road overlook the sea, while Nissaki's main attraction, tiny, but exquisite crescents of white shingle, are reached down a surfaced lane. The luxurious Nissaki Beach Hotel, signposted from the main road, has a beach directly below it with numerous facilities that can be enjoyed by non-residents.

✈ 131 D5 ✉ 24km (15 miles) north of Corfu Town, on the main coast road
🍴 Tavernas (€€) 🚌 Green bus from Avramiou Street, Corfu Town–Kassiópi
🚤 Excursion boats from neighbouring resorts ❓ Limited parking

PANTOKRÁTORAS (MOUNT PANDOKRATOR)

See pages 40–41.

PERÍTHEIA (OLD PERÍTHIA)

In the hidden hollows of Mount Pandokrator's upper slopes lie the ruins of old farmsteads and villages. They were established originally by Corfu's Byzantine peoples fleeing repeated pirate raids on their coastal settlements. Abandoned villages can also be found at Old Siniés and at Rou on the east side of the mountain, but Períthia is the most impressive. Today, it is being brought back to life as ruined houses are being renovated, and summer tavernas cater for visitors.

Períthia is reached by the mountain road from Néa (New) Períthia, which lies on the coast road between Kassiópi and Acharávi. About 5km (3 miles) along this mountain road from Néa Períthia, a rough track leads off left from a steep right-hand bend on the surfaced road. (This track eventually joins the road from Strinýlas to the summit of Mount Pandokrator). For Old Períthia, keep on the surfaced road to an old church at the entrance to the village, where there is limited parking.

The framework of Períthia survives within its setting of terraced fields and scattered stands of cherry, almond, oak and walnut trees. Empty houses retain their shutters and tiled roofs, but where doors and windows gape, and floorboards sag alarmingly, it is dangerous to enter.

✚ 131 C5 ✉ 50km (31 miles) from Corfu Town on northern slopes of Mount Pandokrator. Reached from coast road at Néa Períthia 🍴 Tavernas (€€) ❓ Limited parking by road end

RÓDA

North-coast Róda is a pleasant resort with safe
bathing and a handful of tavernas and clubs. A little
harbour within a rough breakwater marks the original
fishing village, and fishing caiques still work from
here. Róda's beach, narrow and sandy, with rocky
patches, is backed by tavernas, cafés, gift shops and
clubs. Part way up the main street is the Church of
Ágios Geórgios, set in an attractive square dotted
with lemon and plane trees. On the inland side of
the main road towards Acharávi (➤ 72) are the
remains of a 5th-century Doric temple to Apollo.
➕ 130 B2 ✉ On the north coast, 37km (23 miles) north of
Corfu Town 🍴 Cafés and tavernas (€–€€) 🚌 Green bus
from Avramiou Street, Corfu Town–Róda ❓ Limited parking
at seafront

SIDÁRI

There are a number of good beaches at Sidári.
Halfway along the long main street is a little village
square, a brave fragment of old Sidári amid the glare of tourism.
There are seats, a seahorse fountain and a bandstand wreathed in
bougainvillaea and geraniums. On the north side of the square is
the cream and white Church of St Nicholas, its porch hung with
lamps and with an icon painted on its domed interior.

At the northern end of the main street a bridge crosses the
Loxida River and the road beyond runs west past villas and hotels.
Lanes between the buildings on the north side lead to beaches
which all claim to be the location of the famous Canal d'Amour. The
image of this 'Channel of Love' has worn as thin as the original sea
arch that gave rise to the name and which has long since collapsed.
Tradition claimed that if you swam through the arch, romantic
events would result. Today, the official Canal d'Amour is said to be
an eroded inlet at the most easterly beach on the north-facing

coast. But some say it is the channel between sea stacks further west, where the beaches of Vithismeno, Apotripiti and Atri vie for attention.

🔢 128 B4 ✉ 36km (22 miles) from Corfu Town on the north coast

🍴 Cafés and tavernas (€–€€)

🚌 Green bus from Avramiou Street, Corfu Town–Róda–Sidári

⛴ Excursions by boat to Kassiópi, Paleokastritsa and the Diapondía Islands, sea conditions permitting

❓ Parking behind the main street. Main street is one way

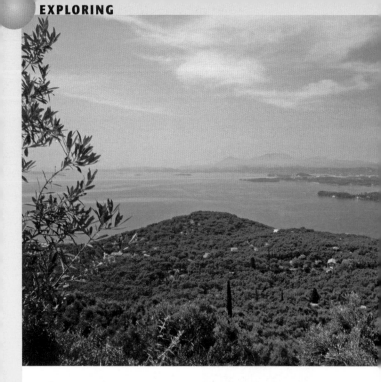

ÝPSOS (IPSOS) AND PYRGI (PIRGI)

The resorts of Ipsos and Pirgi are at the heart of Corfu's so-called 'Golden Mile', and are deservedly popular because of it. They are effectively merged by a long main strip of cafés, restaurants, tavernas, bars, discos and shops on the inland side of the busy main road that skirts Ipsos Bay. An attractive harbour marks the southern end of the resort, and the rugged slopes of Mount Pandokrator make a handsome backdrop. Favoured by the young, the resort is a lively place with a reputation for all-night clubbing. However, the facilities and the safe bathing also make it a good beach for families with young children.

✚ 130 E4 ✉ 15km (9 miles) north of Corfu Town on the coast road 🍴 Cafés and tavernas (€–€€) 🚌 Green bus from Avramiou Street, Corfu–Pirgi–Ipsos 🛥 Small boats for rent and excursion boats

Northwest and Central Corfu

The northwest is an area of discovery, where roads can lead enticingly to invigorating beaches, or to the very edge of towering cliffs.

While there are plenty of family-friendly holiday resorts, it is an area that attracts those who like to get off the beaten track as well as lie on the beach. The northwest outposts of Greece, the Diapondía Islands, are clustered off this stretch of coast, and can easily be reached on a day trip by ferry.

Central Corfu boasts the beautiful west-coast resorts and the remoteness of tree-covered mountains. A rental car is a good idea for this area of Corfu, as it will allow you to explore the spectacular coasts as well as the inland villages, some seemingly untouched by time and tourism.

AFIÓNAS

The road ends at Afiónas. Go any further and you would fall into the sea. To the south of the village lies a narrow promontory that ends at Ákrotírio (Cape) Aríllas, while to the west lies Kravía (Gravia) Island, the 'Ship Island', with its little flotilla of offshore rocks. Just in front of the church at Afiónas, a surfaced lane leads off towards the cape. At a junction, the lane bears right (signed to Dionysos Taverna). Take the left branch along a track that leads out onto the promontory and down to a narrow neck of land at Porto Timoni. Here, small beaches lie to either side. On the headland are the faint remains of walls, which date from 500BC.

➕ 128 D2 ✉ On the headland on the northwest coast 🍴 Three Brothers Taverna (€€) just before entrance to village 🚌 Green bus from Avramiou Street, Corfu Town–Magouládes–Afiónas. Not Sun ❓ Limited parking, especially mid-morning and early evening

ÁGIOS GEÓRGIOS (NORTHWEST)

Ágios Geórgios is an attractive northwest coast resort and although its individuality has been blurred by beachfront development, bold, natural surroundings still dominate the scene. The exquisite sandy beach, framed by tree-clad mountains, sweeps for over 2km (1.2 miles) along the curve of a south-facing bay between Ákrotírio (Cape) Aríllas and Ákrotírio (Cape) Falakron.

Bathing is safe here, although the area can be windy, making the resort a good windsurfing centre. There are windsurfing schools on the beach as well as jet-ski and waterski facilities.

Just inland lies Págoi (Pagi), a traditional Corfiot village, whose narrow lanes were not made for the motor car. Be warned.

➕ 128 D3 ✉ On the shores of the bay on the northwest coast 🍴 Tavernas and restaurants (€–€€) throughout the resort 🚌 Green bus from Avramiou Street, Corfu Town–Ágios Geórgios ❓ Limited parking on beachside road

ÁGIOS STÉFANOS (NORTHWEST)

Corfu's northwest Ágios Stéfanos is a popular family resort, set on the shores of a wide bay with high, white cliffs at the northern end, and a large, flat expanse of beach. The resort, custom-built with villas, hotels, tavernas, bars and shops lining the beachfront, is named after the Chapel of San Stefano, south of the beach. Beyond the chapel is a working harbour full of fishing caiques and excursion boats. There is safe bathing at the beach, and all types of beach equipment are on offer. Water sports include waterskiing and paragliding, and trips can be arranged to the nearby Diapondía Islands (➤ 98) and south to Paleokastritsa (➤ 38–39).

➕ 128 C2 ✉ 45km (28 miles) from Corfu Town on the northwest coast
🍴 O Manthos (€€) 🚌 Green bus from Avramiou Street, Corfu Town–Sidári–Ágios Stéfanos 🚢 Trips to Diapondía Islands and to Paleokastritsa ❓ Some parking on beach

ANGELÓKASTRO

See pages 26–27.

ARÍLLAS

This pleasant resort lies at the northern end of a long bay on the northwest coast of the island, just a few kilometres north of Ákrotírio (Cape) Aríllas. Although remote, there are plenty of resort attractions and gift shops crammed into the narrow approach road.

The narrow beach is mainly sand with patches of shingle and it has a gentle slope into the sea. The bay here can be quite breezy at times, making the resort particularly popular with windsurfers. Boards, pedaloes and canoes can be rented.

Kravía (Gravia) Island lies to the south. Like every other rocky islet off Corfu's coast, it is claimed to be the Phaeacian ship turned to stone by Poseidon in revenge for the Phaeacians transporting Odysseus home to Ithaca.

🚻 128 C2 ✉ 43km (27 miles) from Corfu Town on northwest coast. Reached from Troumbetas 🍴 Several tavernas and cafés (€–€€) 🚌 Green bus from Avramiou Street, Corfu Town–Afiónas, continues to Aríllas 🚤 Excursion boats to and from other resorts ❓ Some seafront parking

DIAPÓNTIA NISIÁ (DIAPONDÍA ISLANDS)

Corfu's Diapondía Islands are the northwest outposts of Greece. The nearest of the three inhabited islands is Mathráki, just under 5km (3 miles) from the Corfu coast. The two others are Eríkoussa and Othoní.

The Diapondías have a long history; flint tools of the early Stone Age, the neolithic and the Bronze Age have been discovered on all of them, and for centuries they were important refuges for ships. At times they were also probably home to pirates. Othoní, the largest of the group, is claimed by some to be Calypso's island from which Odysseus eventually escaped, only to be shipwrecked at Érmones (► 100–101), on the coast of ancient Corfu.

All the islands have beaches and there are some tourist services, including a few tavernas and rooms to let – but choice is very limited. Mathráki is the handsomest of the islands, deeply wooded and with a very long beach. Othoní has several beaches including Aspri Ammos, meaning the 'white sand', on its western shore. Eríkoussa, the busiest of the three, has a long curving beach in front of its main settlement, Porto.

✚ 128 A1 (off map) ✉ 5–15km (3–9 miles) northwest of Corfu 🍴 Mathráki: café (€); Othoní: tavernas (€), restaurant (€€); Eríkoussa: beachside taverna (€) 🚢 Excursions from Sidári and from Ágios Stéfanos (northwest) daily during season, depending on sea conditions. There are regular ferries from Corfu Town and from Ágios Stéfanos. Contact San Stefano Travel ☎ 26630-51910. The crossing can sometimes be quite lively in these open waters

DOUKÁDES

This archetypical Corfiot mountain village lies beneath dramatic limestone crags, with a steep hinterland of lovely olive groves. Viewed from the Troumbetas Pass road, the great cliff above the clustered village seems to hang in mid-air. Doukádes has a pretty central square with adjacent tavernas and shops and there are seats alongside the Church of the Blessed Virgin Mesochoritissa, notable for its splendid doorcases and doors. Numerous Venetian buildings of great style grace the village.

✚ 129 E5 ✉ 18km (11 miles) northwest of Corfu. From the Paleokastritsa road, go through village to a small car park reached down a slip road to the left 🍴 Elizabeth's Taverna (€) 🚌 Green bus from Avramiou Street, Corfu Town–Paleokastritsa, then short steep walk ❓ In late June there is a festival at Doukádes in celebration of St John

ÉRMONES

Picturesque Érmones Bay has a strong claim to being the place where Homer's Odysseus was washed ashore after his voyage from Calypso's isle. Here Odysseus was discovered by the beautiful Nausicaa, daughter of Alcinous, King of the Phaeacians – the legendary inhabitants of Scheria, ancient Corfu.

Érmones lies between two steep headlands, with its shingle beach lapped by dazzling turquoise water. The Rópa River runs into the bay across the middle of the beach and this feature has strengthened the Homeric associations still further. Here Nausicaa and her hand-maidens came to wash clothes 'in the flowing stream of the lovely river', and, while playing a form of classical beach ball, discovered the exhausted Odysseus lying on the beach.

There has been much development of hotels and apartments at Érmones in recent years, and today, beach ball is just one of numerous activities on offer. These include paragliding, and there are several tavernas above the beach.

The beach shelves quickly into deep water and this should always be kept in mind when young children and poor swimmers are swimming in the sea at Érmones.

A rough path leads in a northerly direction from the place where the road ends above the beach, along the northern arm of the bay to the little Church of Zoodochos Pighi (Source of Life). Here there are fine views to a lonely headland.

Situated inland from Érmones, on the green flatlands of the Rópa Valley, is the Corfu Golf and Country Club, where a meandering stream adds a touch of zest to the golf course.

✚ 133 C3 ✉ 17km (10.5 miles) from Corfu Town on west coast. Reached from Rópa Valley, through Vátos ⑪ Nausika Restaurant Bar (€–€€) 🚌 Green bus from Avramiou Street, Corfu Town–Vátos 🚢 Excursion boats to and from other resorts ❷ Limited parking above beach

GLYFÁDA (GLIFADA)

Glyfáda, one of the finest beaches on the west coast of Corfu, with a long stretch of golden sand, is reached down a winding road. There has been much development here and major hotels tend to dominate the backdrop of tree-covered coastal hills. Water sports of every kind are available, and these include sailing and windsurfing. The beach shelves steeply in places, but otherwise Glyfáda is the kind of sandy paradise adored by youngsters. Tavernas line the beachfront and popular venues such as the Aloha Beach Club go non-stop until late into the night. You can find some peace and quiet along tracks and paths to the north and south of the resort.

➕ 132 C4 ✉ 16km (10 miles) from Corfu Town 🍴 Beachside tavernas (€–€€) 🚌 Green Bus from Avramiou Street, Corfu Town–Vátos–Glyfáda 🚤 Excursion boats from neighbouring resorts ❓ Car park behind beach

MAKRÁDES

The little village of Makrádes lies on the road north from Paleokastritsa at the junction with the lane to Kríni and the fortress of Angelókastro (➤ 26–27). Makrádes works very hard at being the retail hub of the known world. Roadside stands and their insistent traders, selling everything from embroidered table linen to knitwear, ceramics and carpets, lie in wait for summer coach parties, while tavernas and cafés help you to get rid of the small change.

Just before Makrádes is Lákones, the village with the view to beat all views. It stands high above Paleokastritsa at the end of a wild series of rising S-bends, with breathtaking views of the west coast.

➕ 128 E3 ✉ 35km (22 miles) northwest of Corfu Town 🍴 Cafés and tavernas (€€) 🚌 Green bus from Avramiou Street, Corfu Town–Makrádes ❓ Roadside parking

MYRTIÓTISSA (MIRTIOTISSA)

Beautiful Myrtiótissa, with its backdrop of tree-covered cliffs, was once a genuine 'desert island' beach, praised by novelist Lawrence Durrell for its 'lion-gold' sand. The south end is favoured by nudists. Difficult access and the cliffs behind the beach have discouraged permanent development – the only blot being the line of telegraph poles and wires that lead to the **Monastery of the Blessed Virgin Myrtiótissa.** It was founded in response to the discovery, in a myrtle bush, of an abandoned icon of the Virgin. The monastery has fine arched doorways and carved keystones, which contrast with the food cans used as flowerpots in the forecourt. The beach shelves slightly and there are offshore reefs and rocks of very rough conglomerate. Beware of currents running offshore.

✚ 132 C4 ✉ 12km (7.5 miles) west of Corfu Town. Reached down a 1km (0.5-mile) track, signposted from the Glyfáda road, or by a 2.5km (1.5-mile) path from the village of Vátos ⑪ Snack bar on beach (€) summer only and Myrtiótissa restaurant (€) uphill from the beach ⑬ Green bus from Avramiou Street, Corfu Town–Vátos ⑭ Excursion boats arrive from other resorts ❓ Parking at beach is very limited

Monastery of the Blessed Virgin Myrtiótissa
🕐 Daily 8–1, 5–8

PALAIOKASTRÍTSA (PALEOKASTRITSA)

See pages 38–39.

PÉLEKAS

This hilltop village has evolved into something of an inland tourist resort due to the popularity of nearby Glyfáda on the coast and of small beaches, such as Kontoyialos and Gialiskari. Above the village is a famous viewpoint, known variously as the Kaiser's Lookout, Tower or Throne, up a steep road signposted from the centre of Pélekas. It was a favourite spot of the German emperor Kaiser Wilhelm II in the early 20th century. The views are spectacular; east to Corfu Town; northwest along the Rópa Valley; south to Mount Ágios Matthéos; and west to the western sea.

Pélekas itself retains the charm of a typical Corfiot hill village, although development has begun to erode its traditional character. There are several tavernas and cafés, plus numerous shops and tourist agencies. In the central square, with its war memorial and well-kept church, an old sea mine serves as an eccentric plant pot.

✚ 132 C4 ✉ 13km (8 miles) from Corfu Town on west coast 🍴 Jimmy's (€€) 🚌 Blue bus No 11 from San Rocco Square, Corfu Town–Pélekas ❓ Limited parking in village. Parking at viewpoint

PEROULÁDES

Corfu's northwestern limits are marked by the dramatic white cliffs of Ákrotírio (Cape) Drástis, near the village of Perouládes, which rise sheer from the sea to heights of over 50m (165ft) in places. Long, narrow fins of rock jut out from the shore and gentler promontories, patched with scrub, mark the far points of land. From the village square, complete with old water pump, a narrow road runs west between huddled buildings. A few metres along the road a lane runs steeply uphill to the right, leading past the village school and church and on to Ákrotírio Drástis. Although the lane is surfaced at first, it soon becomes very rough, and driving along it is not advised. The track leads in about 1.5km (1 mile) to a dramatic viewpoint overlooking the Diapondía Islands (▶ 98) to the northwest. The narrow road at Perouládes leads through the village to a right turning, signposted Longas Beach. This leads shortly to the Panorama Taverna, from where concrete steps descend to a narrow beach below towering cliffs.

✚ 128 B3 ✉ 45km (28 miles) from Corfu Town on northwest coast
🍴 Panorama Taverna (€€) 🚌 Green bus from Avramiou Street, Corfu Town–Sidári–Perouládes–Ágios Stéfanos ❓ Limited parking in village. Parking above Longas Beach

Southern Corfu

The low-lying southern part of Corfu is less developed for tourism than the north and it has long stretches of peaceful beaches, though there are a few big resorts, including the lively, party resort of Kávos. Inland, this is more of a farming area, populated with fascinating villages where the life of Old Corfu goes on unhindered.

Rental bikes can be used for the many off-road tracks on Corfu. Some of the least hilly areas are in the south, around Lake Korissión and Lefkímmi, but, anywhere on the island, you should be prepared for rough surfaces, pot-holes and steep climbs. The southern tip of Corfu, Akrotíro (Cape) Asprókavos, is the recommended starting point for the Corfu Trail, a 200km (124-mile), fully marked walk crossing the whole island, detailed in *The Companion Guide to the Corfu Trail* by Hilary Whitton Paipeti or on the website (**www.**corfutrail.com).

ACHILLEÍO (ACHILLEION PALACE)

See pages 22–23.

ÁGIOS GEÓRGIOS (SOUTHWEST)

Like its northern namesake, this Ágios Geórgios has been tacked on to a long stretch of sandy beach, part of the almost continuous 12km (7.5-mile) strand that fringes the southwest coast of Corfu. Linear development has left the resort without much heart, but location is what matters. Numerous water sports are available and there are several good tavernas overlooking the beach. The beach is narrow, but you can find uncrowded space if you are willing to walk along the open coast in either direction.

On the main road, inland, is the village of Argyrádes (Argirádes), worth visiting for its Venetian architecture, its shops and cafés.

➕ 134 D3 ✉ On the southwest coast 🍴 Several good restaurants and tavernas (€–€€) or Kafesas (€€€) for seafood at the south end of the resort 🚌 Green bus from Avramiou Street, Corfu Town–Argirádes–Ágios Geórgios ❓ Limited roadside parking

ÁGIOS GÓRDIS

This is an attractive west-coast resort at the foot of spectacular pine-covered coastal hills. The beach is framed by big headlands to north and south; at the northern end are Plitiri Point and the rocky heights of Aerostato, known at one time as 'The Lookout' because of its use as a watch-point for pirates and potential invaders. Just offshore from Ágios Górdis's southern headland is a remarkable tusk-like pinnacle called the Ortholith. Onshore is a similar pinnacle, beyond which rises Mount Garoúna. The beach is wide and sandy with patches of shingle, and numerous water sports are available, including a beachside diving centre. A steep hike to the south from Ágios Górdis takes you to the rocky cove of Fieroula and on to the hamlet of Pentátion.

✚ 133 E5 ✉ 17km (10.5 miles) southwest of Corfu Town 🍴 Cafés and tavernas (€–€€) throughout resort 🚌 Green bus from Avramiou Street, Corfu Town–Ágios Górdis ❓ Limited parking at beach, but car park before road end

ÁGIOS MATTAÍOS (ÁGIOS MATTHÉOS)

There is an enduring belief that in Ágios Matthéos local people are descended from the Byzantine defenders of nearby Gardíki Castle (► 114–115).

The village, one of the largest and most traditional of Corfu's mountain villages, is built on a series of terraces on the tree-covered slopes of the 463m (1,519ft) Mount Ágios Matthéos, known locally as Grava. Near the top of the mountain is the 4th-century Monastery of Pandokrator, now abandoned but still cared for by the villagers. On 6 August each year a religious festival is held here through the night.

A paved lane winds through the heart of the village to a wide square with a fountain and a well-kept church. The view east across the island from here is exhilarating.

✚ 134 A1 ✉ 22km (13.5 miles) southwest of Corfu Town 🍴 Snack bars (€) in main street 🚌 Green bus from Avramiou Street, Corfu Town–Ágios Matthéos ❓ A small car park on the northern edge of the village, signposted

ÁKROTÍRIO ASPRÓKAVOS (CAPE ASPRÓKAVOS)

Beyond the liveliness of Kávos, with its numerous bars and clubs (► 116–117), there is an altogether different world. At the south end of the resort a road branches left to Pantatika, the final beachside extension of Kávos. Beyond, a rough track branches right into olive groves and within seconds you are in a world of shaded trees and peace and quiet – provided it is not the height of the shooting season.

Keep to the main track as it winds on through deep woods of olive, cypress, ilex and oak, towards Cape Asprókavos. It reaches the coast above pale sandstone cliffs and finally leads to the ruin of the ancient Moní Panagiás (Monastery of Panagia Arkoudilla). Here, the Venetian bell-tower survives, framed between tall cypresses. Inside the building there are faded wall-paintings and a handful of icons.

➕ 135 F8 ✉ 50km (31 miles) south of Corfu Town, 2km (1.2 miles) from southern end of Kávos 🍴 Wide choice of snack-bars, cafés in Kávos (€)

🚌 Green bus from Avramiou Street, Corfu Town–Kávos

ALYKÉS (ALIKES)

The Alykés salt pans, reached by road from Áno (Higher) Lefkímmi, lie on the eastern shore of the Bay of Lefkímmi. They were once exploited by the Venetians and now large numbers of migrating birds are attracted to the disused pools in spring and autumn.

✚ 135 C7 ✉ 32km (20 miles) south of Corfu Town via Áno Lefkímmi
🍴 Beachfront taverna (€) at Petrakis ❓ Parking at road end by salt pans

BENÍTSES

There are two Benítses: brash resort and traditional Greek village. Old Benítses is an absolute delight. *Caiques* (light fishing boats), laden with nets, lie with their bows towards the harbour quays. The village square is a mix of Venetian buildings and two-storeyed houses and tavernas. A short distance north from the square, a narrow alleyway (signposted 'Roman Baths') leads to a lemon grove and the fascinating ruins of the bathhouse of a Roman villa. The old village extends inland and amid the citrus trees is a fine old church. The Corfu Shell Museum at the northern entrance to Benítses is worth a visit. It is one of the biggest and best-curated collections of shells from world-wide locations.

Resort Benítses lies south of the old village, beyond the tiny roadside Church of St Dimitrious with its single bell-tower and tiled roof. The resort is a busy social hub during the summer. The resort's reputation has mellowed, although the clubs and bars are still lively. The beach is a narrow shingle strip with the busy main road alongside. All types of water sports are available; a sizeable marina is under construction at Benítses and it should reinvigorate the village.

✚ 133 E7 ✉ 13km (8 miles) south of Corfu Town on the main road
🍴 Paxinos Taverna (€€), just inside the Old Village 🚌 Blue bus 6, from San Rocco Square, Corfu Town–Pérama–Benítses 🚢 Excursion boats ❓ Toilets at village square. Car parking at north and south ends of resort

Corfu Shell Musem
✉ Benítses ☎ 26610-72227 🕐 Daily 10–8 💷 Moderate 🍴 Café (€)

BOÚKARIS

South of Moraïtika and Mesongí the main road swings inland and then runs down the centre of the island. An alternative road south from Messongí hugs the east coast and leads past numerous tiny roadside beaches and rocky coves before turning inland at Boúkaris.

There is a small beach at Boúkaris, which has a jetty, and a beachside taverna with thatched umbrella awnings. A rough track continues south along the coast and can be walked or cycled for about 2km (1.2 miles) to the fishing village of Petrití, where some impressively large trawlers moor alongside small caiques in a busy working harbour.

🚹 134 C4 ✉ 23km (14 miles) south of Corfu Town on minor coast road from Messongí 🍴 Boúkaris Beach Taverna (€–€€) 🅿 Roadside parking

GARDÍKI

The Gardíki region lies between Mount Ágios Matthéos (➤ 110) and Lake Korissión (➤ 34–35) and is home to some remarkable historic remains. The most substantial is Gardíki Castle, a ruined Byzantine fortress, which probably dates from the early 13th century. Near Gardíki Castle on the road from Paramonas and Cape Varka is the Grava Gardíkiou rock shelter, dating from the Upper Palaeolithic period of 20,000BC, a time when Corfu was part of what is now mainland Epirus. During this period, primitive hunter-gatherers used such rock shelters while on hunting trips. Many stone tools and animal bones have been found at Grava Gardíkiou and the site is now accessible to the public. A prominent roadside notice board indicates the site, which is about 400m (1,300ft) uphill through olive groves. Orange arrows, on brown metal signs pinned to the trees, point the way. The cave may seem mundane, but its antiquity creates a powerful sense of the past. Just up the road, a more modest sign indicates an old fountain built by Serbian soldiers in 1916.

Lake Korissión is reached by continuing from the fortress to the scattered hamlet of Gardíki, from where a side road leads to the north end of the lake. A short distance further on from the Lake Korissión turn, a track leads down to the isolated Kanouli and Alonáki beaches. Alonáki has several small fishing boats, which are launched down ramps.

✚ 134 B2 ✉ 25km (15 miles) south of Corfu Town. Reached from the main road 1km (0.5 miles) beyond Messongí

🍴 Alonáki Beach Taverna (€)

🚌 Green bus from Avramiou Street. Corfu Town–Ágios Matthéos. Get off at Gardíki turn, then short walk

❓ Limited roadside parking by castle

KÁVOS

Kávos is Corfu's premier resort for loud and often exhibitionist holidaymaking, although no one is too lively at midday thanks to the previous night's sessions in the dozens of bars and clubs. Kávos is definitely for young, uninhibited adults, with a majority of British among them, and the first thing anyone looking for local colour will notice is the total lack of the Greek language on signs. The resort has effectively overwhelmed itself and its everyday facilities with full-on frantic boozing and partying. The sun rises on some unlovely sights after each night's excess. Not for the fastidious, but definitely for the 'funster', although you need to be fairly sharp yourself to handle a few hard-edged operators. There is a 2km-long (1.2-mile) beach, the plusses being safe bathing and plenty of water sports and other diversions.

An older Kávos survives in the forms of a handful of small fishing boats that keep their distance on offshore moorings. The beach peters out to the south, where low cliffs begin. Beyond are the lonelier reaches of Ákrotírio (Cape) Asprókavos, if you feel in need of some solitude.

🚩 135 E8 ✉ 45km (28 miles) south of Corfu Town at end of main road south
🍴 Snack-bars and tavernas (€–€€) 🚌 Green bus from Avramiou Street,
Corfu Town–Kávos 🚢 Excursion/rental boats ❓ Limited roadside parking

LEFKÍMMI

The far south of Corfu may
have Kávos as a major resort,
but the true character of the
area is epitomized by the town
of Lefkímmi – a straggle of
communities, including
Melikia, Potami, Anaplades
and Ringlades, that have
merged into one. Lefkímmi,
or 'Ta Lefki' to locals, is the
commercial centre of the
south's farming and vine-
growing area, and reflects
the everyday life beyond the
beaches. Today, Lefkímmi is
bypassed by a two-lane
highway which hurtles south to Lefkímmi Port where it ends at the
entrance to a vast quayside. From here ferries leave for
Igoumenítsa on the mainland and for Paxos (▶ 64–65).

Áno (Higher) Lefkímmi is the first part of the town entered from
the north. By the roadside is the handsome Church of St Arsenios.
Arsenios (AD876–953) was the first Archbishop of Corfu. The south
end of the long main street is dominated by the tall bell-tower of
the Church of St Theodoros. Beyond is Potami, with the attractive
'Kampouli' Square and the River Himaros. The riverside roads lead
to the river-mouth, where there are small beaches and sand dunes.

🚩 135 D7 ✉ 40km (25 miles) south of Corfu Town 🍴 Maria's Taverna,
Potami (€) 🚌 Green bus from Avramiou Street, Corfu Town–Kávos
❓ Roadside parking. Lefkímmi Festival, 8 July

LÍMNI KORISSIÓN (LAKE KORISSIÓN)
See pages 34–35.

MESSONGÍ (MESONGÍ)
Separated from Moraïtika by the Messongí River, Messongí is the first resort south of Corfu Town to escape from the main road. The coast sweeps away in a gentle curve to the south where tree-covered hills fill the horizon. The narrow sand and shingle beach has safe bathing and is ideal for families; a narrow road, with shops and tavernas, leads from the north end to the river bank.

South from Messongí, a coastal road leads to Boúkaris (► 114) past a number of good fish tavernas. Apart from relaxed meals in the evenings, there is very little nightlife. For restless youth, there are the livelier attractions of nearby Moraïtika, while the clubs of Benítses are only 8km (5 miles) to the north.

➕ 134 B3 ✉ 22km (13.5 miles) south of Corfu Town 🍴 Cafés and tavernas (€–€€) 🚌 Green bus from Avramiou Street, Corfu Town–Kávos or Corfu Town–Messongí 🚢 Excursion boats to other resorts ❓ Roadside parking

MORAÏTIKA
The name Moraïtika sounds convincingly Hawaiian and the resort does its best to live up to the image: the beach has lots of exotic palms and thatched umbrellas. The only thing missing is the surf.

Áno (Upper) Moraïtika, a delightful complex of old houses, modern villas, and a couple of tavernas, all swamped in bougainvillaea, is tucked away on the high ground above the north end of the resort. The dusty main road of the resort proper is lined with restaurants, tavernas, bars, clubs, cafés and shops.

Between road and sea is a broad swathe of land, dotted with villas and hotels, that runs down to Moraïtika's long stretch of sun-trapping sand and shingle beach. The southern end of the beach is dominated by the very large Messongí Beach Hotel, which has its own gymnasium, tennis court, swimming pools, restaurants, beach taverna, café and shopping centre. There are water sports in plenty at Moraïtika, including gentler alternatives for children. The beach even has freshwater shower points and a changing stall at its midpoint.

✚ 134 B3 ✉ 20km (12 miles) south of Corfu Town, on main coast road
🍴 Cafés and tavernas on beach and in main street (€–€€) 🚌 Green bus from Avramiou Street, Corfu Town–Kávos and Corfu Town–Messongí
🚢 Excursion boats from beach ❓ Parking in main street

PÉRAMA

Lying on a steep, wooded shoreline beyond the busy suburb of Vrioni, but not out of earshot of the airport across the adjoining Chalkiopoúlou Lagoon, Pérama is the first resort to the south of Corfu Town. Shingle beaches are reached down steep steps from the main road and, in spite of their small size, offer all sorts of facilities and most water sports. Pérama has numerous hotels, bars and gift shops and is well placed for regular bus connections, south to Benítses and beyond, and north to Corfu Town. The Achilleion (► 22–23) and the charming but busy Gastoúri village are only 3km (2 miles) inland to the south.

About 2km (1.2 miles) south on the coast road are the remains of the 'Kaiser's Bridge', an elaborate pierhead built by Kaiser Wilhelm II to facilitate landing from the imperial yacht.

✚ 133 D7 ✉ 7km (4 miles) south of Corfu Town. On main coast road to Benítses ❚❚ Cafés and restaurants (€–€€) 🚌 Blue bus No 6 from San Rocco Square, Corfu Town–Pérama–Benítses ❓ Parking is difficult

PERIVÓLI

This is another of Corfu's down-to-earth farming villages, with its narrow lanes and alleyways, on the main road south. The church is called Agii Saranda (Forty Saints), a name shared with the Albanian port of Agii Saranda, dedicated in honour of 40 Christian soldiers who were martyred for their faith in the 4th century.

Perivóli has a number of traditional *kafenions* and tavernas which only *aficionados* of Greek living will feel at ease in. The village is the gateway to several accessible points on the great sweep of beach that runs down the southwest coast. These include Paralía Gardénos (Vitaládes Beach) reached through Vitaládes, and Paralía Agías Varváras (Santa Barbara Beach), also with beachside tavernas.

✚ 135 D5 ✉ 35km (22 miles) south of Corfu Town, on main road south to Lefkímmi and Kávos ❚❚ Tavernas at Vitaládes Beach and at Santa Barbara Beach (€) 🚌 Green bus from Avramiou Street, Corfu Town–Kávos ❓ Limited roadside parking. Some parking at beaches

SINARÁDES

This is another traditional Corfiot village, part Venetian, part Byzantine, with an authentic flavour of everyday island life. In the main street there is a medieval bell-tower of unpainted stone, its twin bells still in place. The village square is attractive, with huge palm trees, a small bandstand and a fountain adorned with statues of rearing horses. Sinarádes has its own Philharmonic Orchestra and the square is the focus of some excellent local festivals.

A short distance along the main street south from the square is the Church of St Nicholas. Opposite, a signpost points the way up a paved alley to the delightful **Folklore Museum of Central Corfu,** a two-storeyed building reached by a narrow stairway. Part of the

building is a reconstruction of a 19th-century village house, complete with furnishings and utensils. The exhibits include musical instruments, farming tools and traditional costumes.

✚ 133 D5 ✉ 15km (9 miles) from Corfu Town on the west coast

🍴 Cafés and tavernas (€–€€)

🚌 Green bus from Avramiou Street, Corfu Town–Sinarádes–Ágios Górdis

Folklore Museum of Central Corfu

☎ 26610-54962 🕐 All year Tue–Sun 9.30–2.30. Opening hours are flexible 💷 Inexpensive

Index

Acknowledgements

The Automobile Association wishes to thank the following photographers, companies and picture libraries for their assistance in the preparation of this book.

Abbreviations for the picture credits are as follows – (t) top; (b) bottom; (l) left; (r) right; (c) centre; (AA) AA World Travel Library

4l Ferry, Corfu, AA/C Sawyer; **4c** Beach at Kalami, AA/S Outram; **4r** Street in Afionas, AA/J A Tims; **5l** Corfu Town, AA/C Sawyer; **5c** Taverna in Corfu, AA/C Sawyer; **6/7** Ferry, Corfu, AA/C Sawyer; **10** Greek men and women in traditional dress, AA/M Trelawney; **12/13** Flying Dolphin Ferry, hydrofoil, AA/C Sawyer; **14** Corfu Town bus stop, AA/C Sawyer; **15** Car near Myrtiotissa beach, AA/C Sawyer; **17** Letterbox in Corfu, AA/C Sawyer; **20/21** Beach at Kalami, AA/S Outram; **22/23** Achillion Palace façade, AA/S Day; **23** Achillion Palace, AA/S Outram; **24** St Spiridon, Corfu Town, AA/C Sawyer; **24/25** Interior, St Spiridon, AA/M Trelawney; **26** Ayia Kyriaki, Angelokastro, AA/C Sawyer; **26/27** Angelokastro, AA/C Sawyer; **28** Shuttered buildings, Corfu Town, AA/C Sawyer; **29** Back street, Corfu Town, AA/C Sawyer; **30/31** The White House, Kalami Beach, AA/C Sawyer; **31** Lawrence Durrell photograph, AA/C Sawyer; **32** Vlacherne Convent, Kanoni, AA/C Sawyer; **32/33** Kanoni Peninsula, view towards Vlacherne monastery, AA/C Sawyer; **34/35t** Lake Korission, AA/C Sawyer; **34/35b** Lake Korission, AA/C Sawyer; **36** Lion of Menekrates, Archaeological Museum, Corfu Town, AA/C Sawyer; **37** Mon Repos room, Archaeoogical Museum, AA/C Sawyer; **38** Palaiokastritsa Monastery, AA/C Sawyer; **38/39** Palaiokastritsa, AA/C Sawyer; **39** Palaiokastritsa bay, AA/C Sawyer; **40** Mount Pandokratos, AA/J A Tims; **40/41** Mount Pantokratoras, AA/C Sawyer; **41** View from Mount Panokratoras, AA/C Sawyer; **42/43** Afionas, AA/J A Tims; **45** Corfu Town, AA/C Sawyer; **46/47** Paleopolis, Church of St Jason, AA/C Sawyer; **48/49** British Cemetery, Corfu, AA/C Sawyer; **50/51** Municipal Art Gallery, Corfu Town, AA/C Sawyer; **51** Orthodox Cathedral of Panagia Spiliotissa, AA/J A Tims; **52** Mons Repos Palace, AA/C Sawyer; **52/53** Mon Repos Palace, AA/C Sawyer; **54** Byzantine Museum, Corfu Town, AA/C Sawyer; **55** Cannon on New Fortress, Corfu Town, AA/S Outram; **56** Tomb of Menekrates, AA/S Outram; **57** The Maitland Rotunda, Corfu Town, AA/C Sawyer; **58** Fisherman, New Port, Corfu Town, AA/S Day; **58/59** Fortress and Church of St George, Corfu Town, AA/C Sawyer; **60** Palaiopolis, AA/S Day; **61** Museum of Asiatic Art, AA/C Sawyer; **62/63** Old Port Area, Corfu Town, AA/S Outram; **63** Agios Spiridon, Corfu Town, AA/C Sawyer; **64/65** Orkos, Paxos, AA/A Souter; **66** Venetian Town Hall, JAA/M Trelawney; **66/67** Statue of Polylas, Corfu Town, AA/S Day; **67** First National Bank of Greece, Corfu Town, AA/M Trelawney; **68** San Rocco Square, A/S Day; **68/69** San Rocco Square, AA/S Day; **69** Monastery at Platitera, AA/S Outram; **70** The Liston, Corfu Town, AA/C Sawyer; **71** Agios Stefanos bay, AA/C Sawyer; **72** Almiros beach, AA/J A Tims; **72/73** Antinioti Lagoon, AA/C Sawyer; **74/75** Agios Stefanos harbour, AA/C Sawyer; **75** Agni harbour, AA/C Sawyer; **76/77** Beach at Dassia, AA/C Sawyer; **78/79** Cape Asprokavas, AA/S Day; **79** Ano Korakiano, Venetian House, AA/S Day; **80** Beach at Avalaki, AA/C Sawyer; **80/81** Beach at Avalaki, AA/C Sawyer; **82/83** Dassia beach, AA/J A Tims; **84/85** Beach at Kassiopi, AA/C Sawyer; **86** Kontokali, remains of boatyard, AA/J A Tims; **86/87** Kouloura Bay, AA/C Sawyer; **88** Perithia, Mount Pandokrator, AA/S Outram; **88/89** Perithia, church, AA/S Outram; **90/91** Nightlife in Sidari, AA/C Sawyer; **91** Church in Sidari, AA/S Outram; **92** Ipsos Bay, from Mount Pantokratoras, AA/J A Tims; **93** Pelekas, AA/J A Tims; **94** Afionas, AA/J A Tims; **94/95** View of Agios Georgios, Afionas, AA/C Sawyer; **96/97** Arillas beach, Afionas, AA/J A Tims; **98** Diapontia Islands, AA/C Sawyer; **98/99** Doukades, AA/C Sawyer; **100/101** Beach at Ermones, AA/S Day; **101** Aqualand, near Ermones, AA/C Sawyer; **102/103** Beach at Glyfada, AA/C Sawyer; **104** Telescope, Kaiser's Throne, AA/S Outram; **105** Pelekas, village, AA/M Trelawney; **106** Peroulades, AA/S Outram; **107** Beach at Moraitika, AA/S Outram; **108/109** Windsurfing, Photodisc; **110/111** Agios Mattheos, AA/S Day; **113** Benitses, traditional housing, AA/C Sawyer; **114/115** Gardiki, AA/S Outram; **116** Nightlife in Kavos, AA/C Sawyer; **117** Church, Lefkimmi, AA/C Sawyer; **118/119** Beach at Messongi, AA/S Outram; **119** Harbour at Moraitika, AA/S Outram; **120** Aelos Beach, near Perama, AA/M Trelawney; **121** Church of the Forty Saints, Perivoli, AA/S Outram; **122t** History and Folklore Museum, Sinarades, AA/S Outram; **122b** History and Folklore Museum, Sinarades, AA/S Outram; **123** Taverna, AA/C Sawyer

Every effort has been made to trace the copyright holders, and we apologise in advance for any accidental errors. We would be happy to apply the corrections in the following edition of this publication.

128

129 130 Pandokratoras 131

Kalami

Angelokastro

Paleokastritsa

Campiello
Agios Spyridonas
Mouseio Archaiologiko

Kerkyra
136

132 133 Kanoni

Achilleio

Limni
Korission

134 135

★ Best places to see
■ Featured sight
☐ Kérkyra
(Corfu Town)
☐ Northern Corfu
☐ Northwest &
Central Corfu
☐ Southern Corfu

0   .5 km
0   1 mile

Akr Ag Spiridonas

Orm Aspraou

N Perithia

Loutses

Perigori

Anapaftiria

Kellia

Kato Vodolakos

Akr Kassiopis

Orm Bolana

Akr Varvaras

Kassiopi

Avlaki

Serpa

Ag Georgios

Bralatika

Leondari

Agios Stefanos

Perithia

Tsitsatika

Kokkini

Sinies

Sanda

P Kerasia

906m
Pandokratoras

Paleo Horio

Rou

Vigla

Plagia

Kouloura

Vor Steno Kerkiras

Vinglatouri

Katavolos

Kendroma

Gimari

Kalami

Apolisies

Agni

Nisaki

A

B

C

D

E

F

Tzavros

5 6 7 8

Orm Gouvion
■ **Gouvia**

A

Gouvino

■ **Kondokali**

Kira
Hrisikou

Vidos

24

Orm Potamou

Evropouli □ **Potamos**

KERKYRA ■

Akr Sidero

B

Afra □

Orm Garitsas

□ Ag Ioannis

Alepou □

Potamos

Garitsa

□ Ag Triada

L. ⊁ ✈
Halkiopoulou

■ **Palaiopolis**

Kombitsi □

□ Ag Eleousa

C

□ Kastania

★ **Kanoni**

Hrisiida □

□ Varipatades

Viros □

□ Kalafationes

■ **Perama**

Kouramades □

Ag Prokopios □

25

D

Kastellani □

□ **Kinopiastes**

■ **Sinarades**

287m ▲

Ahillio □

□ Kamara

★ **Achilleio**

Alepohori

□ Ag Deka

Agios Gordis

576m ▲
Ag Deka

■ **Benitses**

E

□ Ano Garouna

Kato Garouna □

holeto

□ Loukata

□ Pendati

□ Dafnata

462m ▲

askia

□ Kato Pavliana

□ Komianata

Ano Pavliana □

□ Kornata

□ Vouniatades

425m ▲

F

□ Strongili

5 6 7 8

Ag Ioannis □

134

Paramonas □

Notes

Notes

Notes

Notes

Notes

Notes

Notes

Notes